SOLVING
CRIME AND DISORDER PROBLEMS

SOLVING
CRIME AND DISORDER PROBLEMS

Current Issues, Police Strategies and
Organizational Tactics

Edited by
Melissa Reuland, Corina Solé Brito and Lisa Carroll
Police Exeutive Research Forum

POLICE EXECUTIVE
RESEARCH FORUM

This anthology is published by the Police Executive Research Forum (PERF) as a service to its members and the general public. The opinions and recommendations expressed in this book are those of the authors and do not necessarily reflect those of the PERF membership or staff.

This publication was generously supported by Global Software Corporation.

Printed in the United States of America

Library of Congress Number 2001 135839

ISBN 1-878734-75-x

Cover by Marnie Deacon Kenney
Interior by Elliot Thomas Grant, etg Design

CONTENTS

Organizational Tactics

FOREWORD

The events of September 11, 2001, have changed the role of local police in America—perhaps forever. Local law enforcement faces the challenges of assuming more responsibility in countering domestic terrorism threats while continuing to address crime and disorder. Success will depend on their ability to build on strong community-policing networks for information exchange and to maintain a collaborative problem-solving approach to crime amid high anxiety and crisis. Now more than ever, departments need to adhere to community problem-solving principles to decrease crime and disorder in their communities, increase their departments' efficiency, and strengthen their relationships with citizens.

For years, the Police Executive Research Forum (PERF) has recognized that the key to advancing problem-oriented policing (POP) is to develop opportunities for practitioners to share information about their efforts. In this spirit, PERF has helped maintain a database of POP-related projects, disseminated numerous books on the subject, published a newsletter, provided technical assistance and training, and hosted the annual International Problem-Oriented Policing Conference with hundreds of law enforcement agencies and other organizations from around the world.

PERF is proud to offer this book on problem solving as yet another resource for policing professionals and students; it provides readers with an opportunity to study more closely the concepts presented in our many information forums. We hope this book will stimulate discussion about the future of POP and encourage police agencies around the world to share ideas and knowledge. We also fervently hope it will help the countless creative and dedicated individuals who serve as our nation's line officers to solve seemingly intractable community problems. This book is dedicated to them.

Chuck Wexler
Executive Director, Police Executive Research Forum

viii

ACKNOWLEDGEMENTS

As with any edited volume, a great many people contributed their expertise and energy—under stringent time constraints—to produce a quality publication. First and foremost, we are indebted to the authors who demonstrated (once again, we are sure) they function well under stress to meet short deadlines. These dedicated law enforcement professionals and researchers make tremendous differences in their communities; through this book, we hope to extend their influence to an even broader audience. It is a pleasure to have the opportunity of thanking these individuals for their dedication to improving the safety and quality of life of so many communities.

We are also privileged to have editing support of the highest caliber. We thank Elliot Grant, of etg Design, for his vision, patience and care in designing the book's layout and polishing the text so it shines. We are always grateful for the eagle eye of Martha Plotkin, PERF's director of communications (who never fails to improve a document she has read), and to Marnie Deacon Kenney for designing the perfect, distinctive cover—again. We also relied on expert assistance from PERF staff to cast a critical eye along the way. We thank David Bright, Melissa Cass and Judy Lim for their thorough attention to detail and willingness to drop everything to assist us in our efforts. Finally, we thank Tony Venturoso and Global Software Corporation for their generous support of this publication.

Melissa Reuland
Corina Solé Brito
Lisa Carroll
Police Executive Research Forum
Washington, D.C.

INTRODUCTION

The United States has experienced tremendous changes in the nature of crime and disorder in the last 10 years. Unprecedented declines in crime numbers in the 1990s have been followed by recent dramatic shifts in the types of crime law enforcement agencies must address. The next decade, no doubt, will continue to challenge law enforcement agencies to apply problem-oriented strategies effectively in solving new situations. The chapters in this book testify to the ongoing success of such efforts in addressing some of today's most critical crime and disorder problems; they also presage the achievements of tomorrow.

Chapters were selected in part from core presentations at the 11th International Problem-Oriented Policing Conference held in San Diego, California, in December 2000. Each year, the POP conference (cohosted by PERF and the San Diego Police Department) provides a forum for practitioners and researchers to share their knowledge of community problems, as well as their experiences responding to those situations. Core presentations examine research and practice around timely crime and disorder problems. The POP conference also showcases the best and most innovative examples of problem solving, several of which are printed here for distribution to a broader audience.

In addition to selections from POP conference presentations, staff identified ongoing PERF research projects that are particularly relevant for today's problem-oriented police departments. All these focal contributions are presented in three sections: Current Issues, Police Strategies and Organizational Tactics.

CURRENT ISSUES

The first section's four chapters address topics of particular relevance to many jurisdictions today. While not themselves new, these crime and disorder problems have recently been the subject of intense scrutiny, revealing unique opportunities for law enforcement strategies. In the first chapter, "Made in the USA: A Community Approach to Methamphetamine Use and Production," Susan Pennell and Jack

Drown detail the work of San Diego law enforcement, local and county government, and researchers to address the increasing problem of methamphetamine use and production in their community. Their comprehensive approaches are based on sophisticated data analysis and collaboration among numerous agencies to educate the community and improve criminal justice system responses.

Joanne Archambault and Suzanne P. Lindsay highlight awareness of nonstranger sexual assault in San Diego in the second chapter. Due to a variety of factors discussed, nonstranger sexual assaults now significantly outnumber stranger assaults reported in this area. The chapter describes the department's efforts to educate the community and its officers on preventing these assaults and investigating them more effectively. The authors also present data from a study comparing characteristics of each type of assault to provide information relevant for investigative strategies.

In the third chapter, Sheldon F. Greenberg reviews the challenges police agencies face in examining the "Police Response to People with Mental Illness." Greenberg identifies some causes of the current increases in calls involving people with mental illness and presents innovative solutions developed by departments nationwide to train officers, use nonstigmatizing language and divert people from inappropriate placement in the criminal justice system.

Lorie A. Fridell's chapter focuses on the strengths inherent in working with the community to develop solutions to racially biased policing. Based on work done for a recent PERF project, Chapter Four ("Responding to Racially Biased Policing Through Collaborative Problem Solving") outlines successful approaches using collaboration and the SARA (Scanning, Analysis, Response, Assessment) model. Fridell traces several example problems through the SARA process, detailing specific questions and methods for each stage.

POLICE STRATEGIES

The four chapters in this section demonstrate how effectively the SARA model can be used to address a wide range of problems. Chapter Five presents one winner of the 2000 Herman Goldstein Award for Excellence in Problem-Oriented Policing, "Graffiti Prevention and

Suppression." Corinne Hard, David Tos and Daniel T. Albright used interviews and data collection to gain a thorough understanding of taggers' motivations and practices. The San Diego Police Department's Mid-City Division coupled this knowledge with community policing tactics to reduce graffiti in the area dramatically.

In Chapter Six, Dan Cunius, Eric Rost and Chuck Johnson discuss their solution to Charlotte-Mecklenburg's problem of "Appliance Burglaries from Residential Construction Sites." Officers carefully studied building practices and construction timelines, as well as the relationship between contractors and subcontractors. They then reduced sites' vulnerability and, consequently, theft from them by forging crucial partnerships with contractors to adjust their schedules.

In Chapter Seven, Valerie Spicer and Jean Prince discuss the other 2000 Herman Goldstein Award for Excellence in Problem-Oriented Policing project. The authors highlight initiatives taken by the Grandview-Woodland Community Policing Centre to address the problems of drug dealing and disruptive youth in a public park. "Showdown at the Playground: A Community Confronts Drug and Disorder Problems in a Neighborhood Park" reports how environmental changes to the park, as well as the strong relationship between the community and its police, worked together to improve the situation.

Nigel Manning describes how the Staffordshire, England, Police Department applied its newly espoused problem-solving approach to increased incidents of city begging in Chapter Eight, "Addressing City Begging Using Problem-Oriented Policing." Manning shows how a team of representatives from social services, local businesses, the media and the police department worked together to address the problem and directed beggars to other means of employment.

ORGANIZATIONAL TACTICS

Successful implementation of problem solving relies on transforming several key areas of the agency's organizational approach. The chapters in this section illustrate how agencies can support effective problem solving through changes to their overall approach, information systems and training. Chapter Nine, Stuart Kirby's "Implementation of Problem-Oriented Policing in Lancashire," describes the organizational transformation of the Lancashire, England, Constabulary from a traditional agency to one that applies problem-oriented policing holistically. Kirby discusses how the agency dealt with challenges to implementation and used the SARA model to refine its transformation.

Chapter 10, "Regional Problem Solving Using the National Incident-Based Reporting System," by Donald Faggiani, Daniel Bibel and Diana Brensilber, covers the use of multijurisdictional, incident-based data systems to analyze problems across regions. The authors discuss the advantages of such data systems and highlight the Massachusetts State Police's efforts to analyze drug-related incidents across several regions. The authors also identify several critical data-quality issues that must be addressed by any agency wishing to improve its capacity for using and sharing information across regions.

In Chapter 11, "A New Generation of Field Training: The Reno PTO Model," authors Jerry Hoover, Gerard Cleveland and Greg Saville present the recently developed Reno Police Training Officer (PTO) model for postacademy training. This new model employs adult learning techniques and incorporates problem solving as a fundamental aspect of the program. Developed by the Reno Police Department and PERF, the model focuses on training academy graduates to think as problem solvers rather than call responders.

CONCLUSION

The efforts presented here testify to the hard work and dedication of the many professionals in law enforcement today. Another salient feature of the projects documented in this book is extensive community involvement in successful problem-solving efforts. Now more than ever, law enforcement agencies must turn to their partners to forge long-lasting solutions to crime and disorder problems. We anticipate this publication will serve as a valuable resource to law enforcement agencies, their communities, academics and others committed to problem solving.

1

MADE IN THE USA:

A Community Approach to
Methamphetamine Use and Production

Susan Pennell and Jack Drown

INTRODUCTION

"Meth is an equal opportunity destroyer." An arrestee in a San Diego County jail offered this verdict while responding to a series of questions about his illicit use of the drug methamphetamine. Although the use and production of this drug has historically been confined to the western part of the United States, it began creeping eastward as early as the mid-1990s. Law enforcement agencies and drug treatment providers knew little about the profound consequences of this homemade drug on the environment, the user and individuals around the user. Compared with other illicit drugs, methamphetamine presents different challenges with respect to prevention, intervention, enforcement and treatment. Its unique features suggest that methamphetamine is not solely a police problem, a health problem or an environmental problem; instead, its influence radiates across all three domains.

This article describes how the County of San Diego put research into practice by using a comprehensive community approach to the problem of methamphetamine, hereafter known as meth. The research informing this work is derived from a survey of incarcerated meth users conducted by the San Diego Association of Governments (SANDAG), a long-range planning council of city and county governments with a criminal justice research capability. As part of this comprehensive approach, the County Board of Supervisors created the San Diego Methamphetamine Strike Force to address the meth problem in the area.

Before describing the survey results and Strike Force responses, we will frame the discussion by providing a brief description about the drug, its effects on users and the community, and manufacturing techniques.

What Is Meth?

According to a 1998 report by the National Institute on Drug Abuse (NIDA), methamphetamine is a potent and highly addictive psychostimulant similar to amphetamine (its "parent" drug) and cocaine, in which both the rush and the high are believed to result from the release of high levels of dopamine into areas of the brain that regulate pleasure. Unlike cocaine, however, meth is not metabolized to the same extent; a larger percentage of the drug remains unchanged in the user's body (NIDA 1998). Because tolerance is developed so quickly, users are more likely to indulge in a "binge and crash" pattern (known as "tweaking") in an attempt to maintain the original high, despite the high concentrations that remain in the body (NIDA 1998). Initially, meth users may experience euphoria, as well as increased energy and self-confidence; yet these feelings are short-lived as tolerance develops. Negative side effects accompanying tolerance may include paranoia, tremors, insomnia and irritability. Since meth affects nerve endings, users may over time experience the sensation that bugs are crawling under their skin (called formication) as skin cells die. Prolonged meth use can result in drastic mood swings and violent behavior, along with hallucinations (NIDA 1998).

How Do Meth Laboratories Affect the Community?

Recipes for cooking meth are widely available (Singh 2001). The sale of ephedrine, the primary ingredient, is now federally regulated in the United States but not in many other countries. Also, meth producers have turned to antihistamines and other commercial ephedrine-based products, which they grind to release the meth ingredient. The additional chemicals and ingredients used to make meth (iodine, red phosphorus, hydriodic acid) are extremely toxic and can be volatile. It is not uncommon for the combination of toxic gases and chemicals produced during the cooking process to result in fires and explosions. This creates risks for both neighboring locations and the police who may unknowingly respond to an incident at a meth cooking site. The waste materials or residue from cooking meth can contaminate drinking water supplies, and toxic fumes can permeate through air conditioning units, causing such health problems as headaches, nausea and dizziness (Kansas Department of Health and Environment 2001). Very recently, residue and equipment from meth cookers have been found in national forests around the country.

Who Manufactures Meth?

Meth is unique among illicit drugs because it is homemade—ingredients are readily available and little equipment is needed. In the early 1980s, large-scale production of meth was associated with outlaw motorcycle gangs living in rural areas on the West Coast. As meth became more prevalent and users learned the recipe, more meth was produced by users themselves in small makeshift labs. In the past five years, increasing numbers of Mexican drug traffickers have become involved in meth, using the infrastructure developed by drug cartels for cocaine trade. Ephedrine is not regulated in Mexico, and given the high demand for meth in the United States, Mexican drug traffickers' addition of meth was unsurprising. Nevertheless, the proliferation of meth labs continues in the West and has begun to emerge in the Midwest as well (ONDCP 2001).

STRIKE FORCE BACKGROUND

In early 1996, the San Diego Criminal Justice Council—an informal group of criminal justice policymakers and elected officials—heard reports on meth indicators from a variety of sources. Some of these factors included arrests for possession and sales of meth, quantities of meth seized, drug overdose deaths, emergency room episodes, drug treatment admissions, the number of meth labs dismantled and drug testing information from the Arrestee Drug Abuse Monitoring (ADAM) Program (see NIJ 2000 for more information on ADAM). By all accounts, there was no question that the production and use of meth in San Diego County was reaching epidemic proportions (see Figure 1).

In the spring of 1996, a member of the County Board of Supervisors initiated the San Diego Methamphetamine Strike Force to examine the meth problem. More than 70 individuals attended the first meeting, representing an array of agencies, disciplines (e.g., law enforcement, health, schools, prosecution, judiciary, corrections, drug treatment, social services) and levels of government (including federal, state and local). Each agency outlined the effects of meth production and use in terms of incidence, prevalence, consequences and resource allocation.

It quickly became apparent that this problem could not be addressed by one agency, but instead warranted a multidisciplinary, collaborative approach. In that spirit, two co-chairs were appointed: the San Diego County Undersheriff (second-in-command) and the director of the county's health and human services agency. Under their guidance, Strike Force members began to educate each other and the community about the dangers of meth. Although the problem had been identified, more information was needed to direct prevention and intervention efforts, as well as provide appropriate training for personnel in different agencies. The necessary information came from a survey of incarcerated meth users.

SURVEY OF INCARCERATED METH USERS

SANDAG's Criminal Justice Research Division is a clearinghouse for criminal justice research and administers the ADAM program for San Diego. This program, supported by the National Institute of Justice (NIJ), provides an objective measure of drug use among arrested offenders based on a structured interview and collection of a voluntary, confidential urine sample at the time of arrest.

To provide policymakers, law enforcement, educators and treatment providers with insight into users' perspectives of meth abuse, SANDAG requested and received funding from NIJ to supplement the ADAM interview with a 60-question interview administered to offenders who reported using meth within the previous 30 days. The research took place in five western cities, including San Diego; Port-

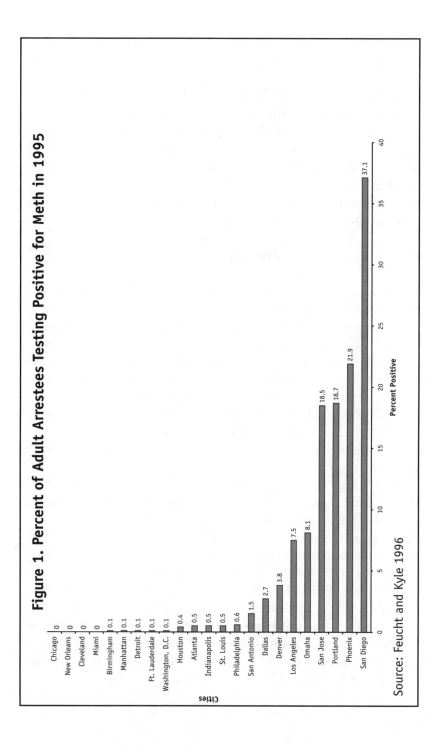

Figure 1. Percent of Adult Arrestees Testing Positive for Meth in 1995

Source: Feucht and Kyle 1996

land, Ore.; San Jose, Calif.; Sacramento, Calif.; and Phoenix, Ariz. More than 1,000 interviews were conducted over 12 months from late 1996 through 1997 with adult men and women and male juveniles. Questions focused on initiation of meth use, patterns of use compared to other drugs, drug treatment experiences, drug market dynamics and meth manufacturing or cooking. Data from the meth addendum were merged with the ADAM data file and analyzed by user characteristics and city. Comparisons were presented between users of other illicit drugs and meth users. The resulting data, discussed in the next section, had important implications for the Strike Force's efforts at prevention, intervention and enforcement (Pennell et al. 1999).

Meth User Characteristics

The study of self-reported meth users arrested and booked into jail revealed that users are primarily white; this was true in all cities except Los Angeles, where Hispanics dominated as users (Pennell et al. 1999). A study conducted in 1997, one year after the Strike Force's inception, indicated that the use of heroin and cocaine was fairly evenly distributed among whites and Hispanics, while blacks were more likely to use crack cocaine (Riley 1997). (The San Diego ADAM site continues to monitor meth use among arrestees, and the findings remain fairly constant over time—with one exception: Proportionately more Hispanics are using meth now than in earlier years.)

Meth users, compared to users of other illicit drugs, are likely to initiate their use at earlier ages and are more likely to use multiple drugs. Another noteworthy difference is that meth users were more likely to report having been previously arrested and incarcerated. An unexpected finding was that meth users were less likely than users of other drugs (16% versus 28%) to be arrested for a violent offense (Pennell et al. 1999). Meth users were twice as likely, however, to be arrested for a drug or alcohol violation. Although the popular perception is that meth causes users to engage in violent behavior—and this indeed has occurred on occasion—these arrest data suggest that acts of violence are *less* likely to be associated with offenders who test positive for meth.

Drug Market Dynamics

Meth users differed from other drug users in that most had a main source supplying the meth. They also were far more likely to buy meth inside a residence and to buy from someone they knew. This is in contrast to the "open-air markets" that have characterized the cocaine and heroin trade.

Patterns of Meth Use

Examining drug use patterns illustrates the severity of use and the different profiles of users. Arrestees were asked how many days in the previous month they had used meth. Across sites, the average number of days varied significantly, from 10.4 days in San Jose to 15.8 days in Phoenix. Consecutive days of meth use (or "runs") ranged from 7.6 days in Portland to 11.7 days in Phoenix (see Figure 2). The most frequent reason given for not using every day was "not a daily or dependent user." Other responses included "wanted to change my life," "needed to sleep" and "health reasons."

Figure 2. Frequency of Meth Use Among ADAM Adult Meth Arrestees, 1996–97*

	Mean Days Used in the Past Month	Consecutive Days Used	Consecutive Days Without Meth
Los Angeles	10.8	8.6	15.8
Phoenix	15.8	11.7	13.6
Portland	10.8	7.6	16.2
San Diego	14.1	10.1	12.6
San Jose	10.4	7.7	14.9
Overall	**13.0**	**9.5**	**14.0**

*Significant at the .05 level

Source: Pennell et al. 1999

The method of meth ingestion is also an indicator of severity of use. In this group, the majority reported snorting or inhaling meth— with the exception of Portland, where nearly half of the users injected meth. Those who injected or smoked meth were more likely than those who snorted to report such consequences as sleeplessness, skin problems, violent behavior and paranoia. In San Diego, over time, meth users have moved toward smoking meth as the most prevalent means of ingesting; this method transmits the drug to the brain quickly and produces a faster high. Smoking meth also can be indicative of more chronic use.

Drug Treatment

Despite the high number of regular meth users, only 28 percent of those interviewed reported ever having been in treatment for their meth use, with ranges from 9 percent in Los Angeles to 34 percent in Portland. When asked why they did not seek treatment, more than 70 percent indicated that they "did not need it" or they "could quit any time" or they "have control over it." These responses may reflect the classic denial of drug users. According to Dr. Alex Stalcup, a nationally recognized expert on drug addiction, this view is particularly dangerous for meth users. Loss of control over meth use can occur rapidly, and users have generally lost control long before they can acknowledge it (Stalcup 1998).

Of those who did enter treatment, more than half did not complete the regimen. Reasons given by users were associated with wanting to use again, getting arrested or getting kicked out of the program. Dr. Stalcup suggests that retention in treatment is particularly difficult for meth users; the drug's effects on brain chemistry can cause triggers that encourage use long after abstinence (Stalcup 1998).

Illegal Drug Activity

Only about one-third of interviewed arrestees admitted to selling or dealing drugs in addition to using meth. Percentages of users engaging in different drug-related activities (e.g., acting as middlemen, packaging and securing chemicals) varied widely across sites, which suggests communities need to examine the scope and nature of meth use, production and trafficking within their borders. Some cities may be distribution points for meth, while other sites are largely manufacturing centers. Proximity to Mexico or Canada, location of interstate highways, housing density, the extent of rural lands and availability of illicit drugs are all factors that can contribute to the scope of a community's drug problem.

The study examined differences between meth users who admitted engaging in selling or dealing illegal drugs and those who reported they did not. Users involved in drug activity

- were younger than other meth users,
- made more illegal income and spent more money on drugs,
- were more likely to have arrest charges involving drugs or alcohol,
- were almost four times more likely to report gun possession 30 days prior to the interview and
- revealed far more extensive meth use.

There were 231 individuals who reported either dealing or cooking meth within the year prior to the interview. More than half had been selling meth for more than two years. The primary reasons for dealing were equally distributed between supporting an addiction and wanting to make money. About one-quarter of this subgroup stated they sell meth outside their county of residence. Smaller percentages indicated they sell out of state; half of those sellers were from San Diego. A small number reported selling to individuals outside the United States. When asked what they worry about when dealing drugs, 6 out of 10 said, "getting busted." Precautions taken to avoid getting caught or injured included selling only to friends (51%). More general precautions to avoid injury from other users or sellers included carrying some type of weapon (25%).

Based on the number of individuals sold to and the average amounts sold, it appears the dealers in this study were relatively low-level street sellers and users. This is consistent with the population booked into local detention facilities for state law violations. More sophisticated drug producers and dealers may be less visible to municipal law enforcement agencies, which must respond to thousands of calls for service. Likewise, federal and state narcotics agencies may be more likely to encounter higher-level drug offenders, who eventually get booked into federal correctional facilities.

Implications for Prevention, Intervention, Enforcement and Treatment

The findings of the five-site meth study show that methamphetamine presents unique challenges to practitioners and policymakers alike. Study results and the authors' experience suggest the following salient features about meth use and production, much of which helped shape the response to San Diego County's methamphetamine problem:

- Communities differ with respect to the proportion of meth users to users of other drugs. Meth use has been prevalent in the West for several years.
- Communities vary in terms of the scope of meth production, use and trafficking. Some communities, due to their location, may be primarily distribution centers.
- Meth use and production has far-reaching consequences not only for chronic users, but also for those in proximity to labs who may be exposed to fumes or chemicals that can explode or cause fires. Water supplies may also be affected by waste materials.
- Characteristics of meth users differ from individuals traditionally associated with illegal drug use. Particularly, meth users become addicted quickly and are more resistant to treatment than users of other drugs.
- The meth drug market (with the exception of the involvement of some Mexican drug traffickers) appears to be loosely organized and somewhat "closed," in that users tend to buy from people they know, have a main source and purchase meth at indoor locations.
- As certain chemicals become less available through regulation and dealers attempt to cut their product, meth cookers resort to other substances, such as commercial products that can be bought at warehouse stores and tack and feed establishments.

THE METHAMPHETAMINE STRIKE FORCE

San Diego County has a long history of collaborative efforts to address local issues, particularly in the criminal justice arena. What was innovative about the Strike Force was the scope of participation across different agencies and systems. In addition, given what was learned about meth, top administrators acknowledged the drug is not just a police problem and not just a health issue—it requires the commitment of both justice and health, along with schools and the prevention community.

The California Border Alliance Group (a member of the Strike Force) provided funding for the Strike Force infrastructure through the Office of National Drug Control Policy. Strike Force members interpreted the data indicators about meth and shared their experiences with meth users, dealers and cookers. Within a short time, the group proposed 17 recommendations in the areas of prevention, intervention, treatment, enforcement and interdiction (outlined in the following section). Cognizant of the need to involve and inform the community, a media advocacy effort began immediately. The Narcotics Information Network Division of the California Department of Justice initiated a meth hotline, through which the community could report potential meth labs or dealers anonymously and learn about possible treatments for meth abuse.

The Strike Force comprised three focus teams: research, resource and media. A coordinating committee provided leadership and direction. The resource team sought funding and other resources to implement recommendations and began laying the groundwork for special projects. In a Local Partner Project, for example, one city mustered its forces to address meth in much the same way as the county task force (albeit on a smaller scale). The research team began exploring the scientific literature on meth to find out "what works" with respect to treatment for meth users. The media team was tasked with keeping the meth issue in the forefront of the public eye by developing regular news stories about meth.

Before long, local news reporters were identifying criminal incidents in which meth could have been a factor; three particular stories caught the attention of the national media. One involved an individual who confiscated a military tank and proceeded through residential neighborhoods slamming into parked cars. Once on a major cross-town freeway, the suspect—who was later found to be under the influence of meth—rammed vehicles until stopped and killed by police. In another incident, a man who was high on meth commandeered a local transit bus and drove around town for several hours before police subdued him. Finally, a horrific incident involved a four-year-old girl who was scalded in the bathtub by her aunt and uncle, who were high on meth. The child later died.

The media team also designed billboards that asked "What's Cooking in Your Neighborhood?" The billboards provided the telephone number of the meth hotline and were displayed in several prominent locations countywide. This billboard design was subsequently adopted by Phoenix, Ariz., and Salt Lake City, Utah.

ACCOMPLISHMENTS IN ADDRESSING THE METH PROBLEM

From 1996 to 2000, San Diego instituted a number of efforts to address meth production and use. Though not responsible for all of these, the Strike Force certainly contributed to their implementation. Efforts focused on improving education, changing the criminal justice system response, passing legislation, enhancing community treatment and conducting research.

Improving Education

Community education efforts included two conferences on meth, featuring local and national experts who discussed the consequences of meth use and possible solutions. Both one-day conferences were well attended, with more than 200 educators, police officers, medical personnel, social service providers and judges.

In addition, several education materials were prepared to increase the general public's awareness of methamphetamines. One documentary video depicted actual users in recovery and presented compelling data from the ADAM program; it was distributed to schools to inform youth of the dangers of meth use. A local freelance reporter developed a video that included graphic descriptions about the consequences of meth use, as well as film footage of the meth user driving the stolen military tank (described in the previous section). The video also presented expert testimony about the ways meth affects brain chemistry and the barriers to full recovery. This video was aired on local public television and shared at national meth meetings.

As another part of educating the public, the media team ensures that at least one major meth story hits the media at least once per quarter. For example, one reporter stationed outside the medical examiner's office released information on the number of deaths in which meth was a contributing factor. Another story included an interview with a forest ranger who cautioned about the impact of meth waste materials in the mountains and the danger to campers and hikers in national forests. This media coverage reminds the public that methamphetamine is still a serious problem, with far-reaching consequences for both individual health and the environment.

Changing the Criminal Justice System Response

State funding provided the impetus for a multidisciplinary team of police, prosecutors and child protective service workers to assist children exposed to meth cooking. The team is now dispatched when police are called to intervene at a location where meth is being cooked. The children are removed and tested for exposure to toxic fumes.

In recognition of the ease with which users can acquire the ingredients of meth, the San Diego U.S. Attorney's Office, along with local law enforcement, held discussions with such warehouse stores as Wal-Mart and Costco to restrict bulk sales of specific over-the-counter drugs. The office developed and distributed a brochure to store managers/owners, providing them with information on equipment used to make meth, ingredients (such as Sudafed and iodine) and legal restrictions on bulk sales of these items.

The city of Vista (in northeastern San Diego County) implemented the Vista Partner Project, which includes a component called Operation Housecall. Sheriff's deputies identify meth users who are in jail; after their release, the deputies contact them at home to monitor—through conversation and observation—their compliance with probation orders, as well as encourage them to attend treatment (County of San Diego 2000). Noncompliance with treatment plans may be considered a violation of probation. This effort seeks to help meth users become clean and sober, which will result in fewer illegal activities that support addictions, such as burglary.

Passing Legislation

San Diego County officials successfully lobbied the California legislature to pass enhancement legislation that added child endangerment penalties to specific drug law violations. Both the City and County of San Diego also enacted ordinances to regulate specific precursor chemicals used to make meth.

Enhancing Community Treatment

The county added a total of 400 residential and nonresidential treatment slots. In addition, the Behavioral Screening and Intervention (BSI) services instrument was implemented in three local hospitals to identify illegal drug users and offer intervention services. Early intervention of this type is associated with reductions in future drug use and reliance on crime to support addiction.

Conducting Research

SANDAG researchers and a local drug treatment center (the EYE Crisis and Counseling Center) successfully competed to be part of a seven-site meth treatment replication study of the Matrix treatment approach. This approach uses a cognitive-behavioral, outpatient treatment model developed by the University of California–Los Angeles Drug Research Group. The Substance Abuse and Mental Health Services Administration (SAMSHA) funded this three-year research study to determine if Matrix is more effective than current methamphetamine treatment methods.

Members of the Strike Force research team held focus groups with individuals in drug recovery centers and developed a report about how intervention and treatment could be better tailored to San Diego County.

The Strike Force also developed a Meth Report Card that is presented periodically to policymakers and practitioners in criminal justice, health and social service organizations (County of San Diego 2000). The report card includes 10 related indicators of meth production and use (e.g., number of meth-related deaths, drug treatment admissions, positive meth test results for adults and juveniles, and number of arrests for meth sales and possession). The report card helps the Strike Force identify the severest problem areas, organize methods to reduce meth-related problems and document changes over time.

Lessons Learned

Through the efforts and accomplishments of the Meth Strike Force, San Diego County learned a number of lessons that directly relate to core elements of its approach. This information may be helpful for other communities that suspect an emerging meth problem. Important considerations for prevention, intervention, treatment, enforcement and interdiction are discussed below.

Prevention

Meth use is directly correlated to early onset of alcohol abuse and use of other drugs (Pennell et al. 1999). Community strategies for prevention must be similarly linked; educators should be aware of risk factors for co-occurring substance abuse. Prevention efforts also should move beyond classroom discussions to influence community norms, the home and the workplace. Such efforts could include community education programs and media involvement (e.g., billboards, public service announcements), both of which have been shown to increase public awareness significantly. Furthermore, prevention efforts must be informed by research on initiation of meth use and ease of obtaining drugs. Information on drug availability is critical to prevention efforts.

Intervention

The use of a brief screening instrument (BSI) in multiple settings (e.g., health clinics, emergency rooms) may help healthcare professionals identify drug users and encourage them to seek treatment. Further expansion of the aforementioned BSI services can provide useful information and referrals to at-risk and dependent patients. With new users (such as youths), parents and the community need to set clear standards with regard to drug use and provide appropriate sanctions to keep youths accountable for their behavior.

Treatment

Meth users are more resistant to treatment than other drug users because of meth's effects on brain chemistry. Research about meth users suggests that long-term treatment is necessary, and aftercare is critical. Meth users have individual needs that require expertise and understanding in the following domains: psychological, dental, medical, legal, social and educational.

Enforcement

Ongoing training for law enforcement is necessary on several specific topics. Law enforcement officers need to be informed about the characteristics of users, the characteristics of meth labs and how to approach potential labs to maximize safety. For example, patrol officers need to know the effects of meth and recognize meth users in the field, particularly those who are also dealing drugs and may be carrying weapons. In addition, chronic use of meth can be associated with extreme paranoia. Meth users who also cook have been known to bolster their living quarters with weaponry and booby traps. Finally, field officers must be vigilant regarding household items associated with meth, especially when there are several in one location (e.g., coffee filters, iodine, tubing and glass containers). Care should be taken, along with appropriate clothing and breathing apparatus, when approaching a potential meth cooking location.

Interdiction

A number of agencies must be involved in any community interdiction effort to address the meth problem. Critical to their success is continuous sharing of information. The recipe for meth changes quickly, as do manufacturing sites and trafficking patterns, and this information needs to be passed on to all concerned participants. If supported with regular media coverage, a telephone hotline can provide tips for police interdiction efforts as well as useful information or referrals for citizens. Communities along international borders are a priority for interdiction efforts because increased smuggling counters local progress toward lab seizures.

CLOSING REMARKS

It is clear that the efforts of the Strike Force have had an impact by raising community awareness about meth, leveraging resources through interagency cooperation and attracting new, methamphetamine-specific resources to the region. The San Diego Methamphetamine Strike Force has made great strides since its inception in 1996, although success is difficult to measure with the current state of indicators of drug use. The membership is committed to staying the course to hold the public's attention, support and commitment to reducing meth problems. The leadership knows that our region's meth problems will not simply vanish, and we continue to learn from our experience by assessment. The model developed in San Diego has received nationwide attention, and several communities across the country have requested information about this approach (County of San Diego 2000).

While the Meth Report Card is presented annually to elected officials and serves as a catalyst for review, trend analysis and future planning, continued assessment is critical. Meth Strike Force members maintain that meth is a persistent and chronic problem in San Diego; no single measure or time period can—or should—direct public policy. With the enactment in California of Proposition 36 in July 2001 (which mandates drug treatment for all first-time arrests for drug possession), the need for drug indicator data is even more important.

Great strides have been taken in the past several years, but more data collection and research are necessary. The ADAM interview data, with the supplementary questions for meth users, must continue and be reported in a timely manner so that law enforcement and treatment practitioners can strategize accordingly. Public health surveillance of meth-specific data must continue and be enhanced to include accidents involving meth, as well as suicides and homicides where meth is identified. More information is needed about initiation of drug use, drug marketing dynamics and appropriate drug treatment for all populations. Finally, more studies are necessary to identify the needs of children and others with passive exposure to meth.

REFERENCES

County of San Diego. 2000. *County of San Diego, Methamphetamine Strike Force—Status Report*. Division of Drug and Alcohol Services, County of San Diego, California.

Feucht, T. E., and G. M. Kyle. 1996. *Methamphetamine Use Among Adult Arrestees: Findings From the Drug Use Forecasting (DUF) Program*. National Institute of Justice. Available online at http://www.adam-nij.net.

Kansas Department of Health and Environment. 2001. *Cleaning Up Former Methamphetamine Labs*. Available online at http://www.kdhe.state.ks.us/methlabs/cleanup.html.

National Institute of Justice (NIJ). 2000. *1999 Annual Report on Drug Use Among Adult and Juvenile Arrestees*. Available online at http://www.adam-nij.net.

National Institute on Drug Abuse (NIDA). 1998. *Methamphetamine Abuse and Addiction Research Report Series*. Available online at http://www.nida.nih.gov.

Office of National Drug Control Policy (ONDCP). 2001. *Pulse Check: Trends in Drug Abuse, Mid-Year 2000*. Executive Office of the President. Available online at http://www.whitehousedrugpolicy.gov/publications/drugfact/pulsechk/midyear2000.

Pennell, S., J. Ellet, C. Rienick and J. Grimes. 1999. *Meth Matters: Report on Methamphetamine Users in Five Western Cities, Research Report*. Washington, D.C.: U.S. Department of Justice.

Riley, J.K. 1997. *Crack, Powder Cocaine, and Heroin: Drug Purchase and Use Patterns in Six U.S. Cities, Research Report*. Washington, D.C.: U.S. Department of Justice, National Institute of Justice and Office of National Drug Control Policy. NCJRS, NCJ 167265.

Singh, D. 2001. *Wyoming's Methamphetamine Initiative: The Power of Informed Process*. Bureau of Justice Assistance, Office of Justice Programs, U.S. Department of Justice. Available online at http://excalib1.aspensys.com/scripts/cqcgi.exe/@ncjrs.env.

Stalcup, A. 1998. Personal observations at a methamphetamine training session. San Diego, Calif.: January 1998.

2

RESPONDING TO NONSTRANGER SEXUAL ASSAULT

Joanne Archambault and Suzanne P. Lindsay

Rape and other forms of sexual assault are crimes of power and control, perpetrated throughout history primarily by men against women. Forcible sexual acts committed against an unwilling person are currently classified and investigated as serious crimes (felonies) by the criminal justice system. In recent years, many police and sheriff's departments—particularly those in large urban areas—have developed specialized sex crime units staffed by officers, detectives and other victim support personnel specifically trained to respond to and investigate reports of sexual assault (Fairstein 1993). Despite these efforts, the criminal justice system's response to a reported sexual assault continues to be challenged and compromised by issues that do not generally apply to other crimes.

First, sexual assault is one of the few crimes reported to law enforcement that still receives intense scrutiny into the "believability" of the victim's description of events. Further, it is probably the only reported crime in which the suspect can offer a successful defense by claiming the victim consented to the crime. Additional factors affecting how these crimes are investigated and adjudicated include the context in which the assault took place, the victim's perceived character, the victim's age, the prior relationship between the victim and the suspect, and the perception of criminal justice practitioners and even victims about what constitutes a real sexual assault.

The following section reviews the nature of sexual assault and how our understanding and the laws against it have changed in recent years. Next, we review the San Diego Police Department's (SDPD's) data collection, analysis and prevention efforts. The SDPD is very involved in educating both the community and law enforcement per-

sonnel about the dynamics of sexual assault. The last section describes
an epidemiological study conducted to 1) provide the SDPD Sex Crimes
Unit with a better understanding of these crimes in San Diego; 2)
identify important differences between stranger and nonstranger
assaults; and 3) investigate the factors associated with the law enforcement outcomes of these cases.

THE NATURE OF SEXUAL ASSAULT: TOWARD A CLEARER UNDERSTANDING OF THIS CRIME

For generations, we have conceived of sexual assault or rape as a
violent and unprovoked attack *by a stranger* on a defenseless, vulnerable and unsuspecting victim—the stranger in the unlit parking lot,
the man with a knife on the jogging path, the hooded man dressed in
black climbing silently into a bedroom window. These are our images
of the crime. Such images are reinforced by the media and even by
those responsible for tracking and monitoring the crime (the FBI's
Uniform Crime Report, for example, captures information only about
forcible rape). Our understanding of this crime as one perpetrated by
an unknown and violent stranger influences (even without conscious
intent) our attempts to investigate and evaluate sexual assaults. But
these images do not reflect the nature of the crime as it is reported
to law enforcement. Sexual assault by a stranger, though certainly a
very real and serious crime, currently represents a minority of sexual
assaults reported to law enforcement.

As shown in Figure 1, data from San Diego support this trend
in reporting. James LeBeau (1988) studied sexual assaults reported
to the SDPD from 1972 to 1976. In four out of five of his study
years, stranger assailants were described in 70 percent or more
of reported sexual assaults. Dr. LeBeau hypothesized that "Assaults
by strangers allow victims to see themselves as classic victims
conforming to the popular conceptions of the crime" (LeBeau
1988, 202). Twenty years later, however, this was no longer true.
Data derived from the SDPD Sex Crimes Unit case logs from 1992
to 1996 show that only 17 to 31 percent of sexual assaults re-

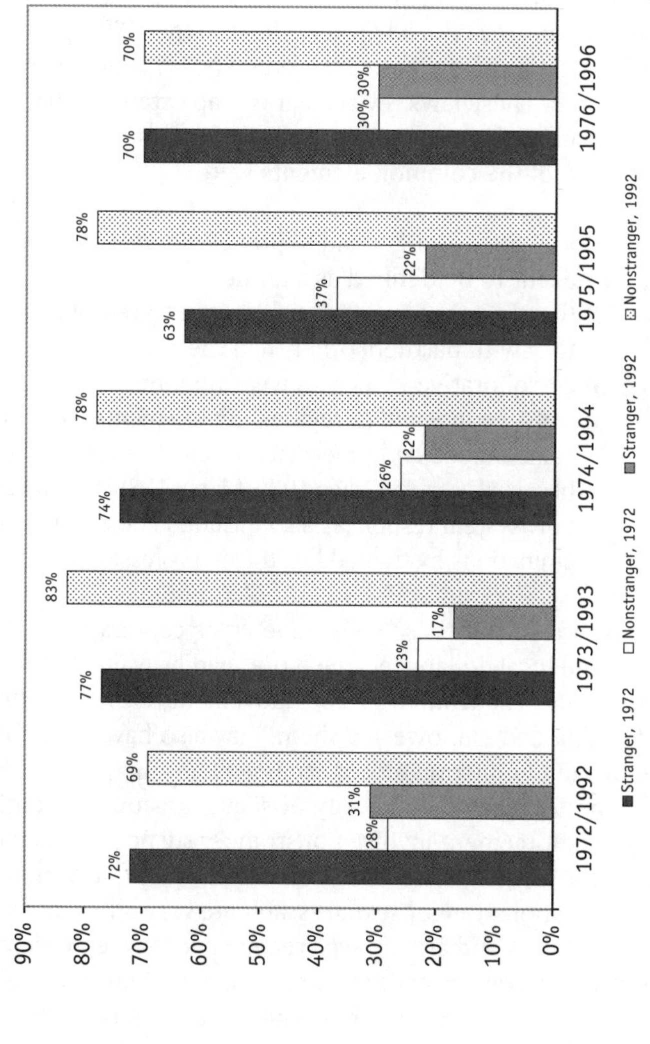

Figure 1. Number and Percent of Sexual Assaults Reported to Involve Stranger and Nonstranger Suspects (1970s vs. 1990s, City of San Diego)

ported to the SDPD in those years involved stranger assailants. In fact, the majority of sexual assaults reported to law enforcement throughout the country currently involve nonstranger suspects (Greenfeld 1997; Bachman and Saltzman 1995).

Many factors together might explain the current high prevalence of nonstranger sexual assault reported to law enforcement. A groundswell of victim advocacy efforts in the 1970s persuaded states nationwide to pass what came to be known collectively as Rape Reform Laws. These laws revised earlier rape statutes that were unnecessarily insensitive to victims. Each state passed its own set of laws, but a few of the common elements were

1) a victim no longer had to prove evidence of resistance for the event to be defined as a crime;
2) the victim was no longer required to reveal prior sexual history with partners other than the suspect;
3) corroborative witnesses were no longer required; and
4) state, county and/or regional requirements were instituted for standardized and timely victim-sensitive responses to a report of sexual assault (Galvin 1985; Marsh 1988; LeBeau 1988). These new system responses also included standardized forensic examinations by trained healthcare professionals.

As a result of these laws, rape crisis centers funded by federal, state and local dollars became more readily available to victims (Burgess 1985). The women's rights movement, including efforts toward educating and empowering them, may also have contributed to the reporting of nonstranger sexual assaults.

The fact that the majority of sexual assaults currently reported to law enforcement involve nonstranger suspects has major implications for investigating and understanding sexual violence. The dynamics of nonstranger sexual assault are very different from stranger sexual assault and are not well recognized. Law enforcement cannot prevent or even investigate sexual assaults appropriately until the true dynamics of each type of assault are understood. Moreover, police officers trained to understand the dynamics of stranger assault will not necessarily know how to *respond* effectively when faced with a nonstranger sexual assault case.

For example, police responses to nonstranger sexual assault may be affected by a mistaken belief that sexual assaults committed by nonstrangers are somehow less traumatic than those committed by strangers. This belief is not supported by the literature (Parrot and Bechhofer 1991; Arata and Burkhart 1996; Katz 1991). Although stranger assaults may tend to be perceived as more physically violent—in that they more frequently involve weapons (Lindsay 1998)—assaults by nonstrangers are frequently physically violent as well, and they also involve the betrayal of trust. "Acquaintance rape is different from stranger rapes and other types of victimizations in that it presents a unique challenge to a woman's belief system" (Gidycz and Koss 1991, 270). In 1991, Katz (264–65) found that women raped by nonstrangers were often "more distressed" and took "longer to feel recovered" than women raped by strangers. Also, the victim of a nonstranger assault may be more harshly judged by her peers, the community and the justice system—from the first responding officers to members of the jury, if any. She may also judge herself to be more at fault. Many of these crimes still go unreported, and very few of those reported ever see successful prosecution. In many cases, the victim recognizes the difficulty in pursuing prosecution and chooses to suspend the investigation.

For the past nine years, the SDPD Sex Crimes Unit has made collecting and analyzing information about reported sexual assaults a top priority. The Unit seeks to better understand the crime and develop appropriate responses to reduce risks and improve the safety of all community members.

SDPD Efforts

Initial Data Analysis

Although the SDPD has been actively involved in problem-oriented policing since 1988, few investigative units have examined ways to practice problem solving or contribute to prevention efforts. To facilitate this, the SDPD Sex Crimes Unit in 1993 began applying traditional crime analysis techniques to reported sex crimes. The Unit's goal was to learn as much as possible about the victims, offenders and assault environment—much as is done for a series of burglaries on an officer's beat. The analysis examined the relationship between the victim and suspect, the age of the victim and suspect, their gender, ethnicity, the type of assault (crime code classification), the geographic and physical location of the assault, the time of day, day of the week, and such other factors as whether a weapon or drugs and alcohol were involved. Data were analyzed for all of 1992.

Nonstranger sexual assaults accounted for 69 percent of the 788 sexual assaults reported to the SDPD that year. It became apparent that prior to the assault, victims could have been much better informed of nonstranger rape risks. Community prevention messages about sexual assault did not contain information to help victims recognize and reduce the risk because of the continued focus on stranger danger. It is uncomfortable for anyone to think that a woman or child is at risk among people we love and trust. Unfortunately, denying the truth and focusing prevention efforts only on stranger assault perpetuates the problem and increases the risk of sexual assault to all citizens.

Problem Analysis Advisory Committee

As a result of the preliminary sex crimes analysis in 1993, the SDPD Sex Crimes Unit hosted a Problem Analysis Advisory Committee meeting to brainstorm possible law enforcement responses. Attendees included representatives from law enforcement agencies, medical and military personnel, rape crisis centers, women's resource centers, school personnel and regular SDPD Advisory Committee members. The stakeholders overwhelmingly agreed that the response should be to develop and initiate community education efforts addressing nonstranger sexual assault, with the hope that people would gain insight into the true dynamics and risks surrounding sexual assault in the 1990s.

Because the criminal justice system has historically failed sexual assault victims by focusing on victims' characteristics and social behavior rather than assailants' criminal behavior (Spears and Spohn 1997), this response was initially disturbing to some women's groups and rape crisis centers. They feared any efforts focusing on changing victim behavior would undermine the Rape Reform Laws' premise that victims are not responsible for the crimes committed against them. We worked hard to establish credibility with these groups, clarifying our position by focusing on the realities of the situation. Although we support all long-term efforts to end violence against women, we feel it is the responsibility of law enforcement to provide people with information that can reduce their risk of sexual assault today. This is, for example, the same type of information law enforcement typically provides people to make them less attractive targets for auto theft, burglary and robbery.

One outcome of these dialogues was to eliminate the term "rape prevention" from our vocabulary. Offenders are the only ones who can *prevent* a sexual assault. We maintain, however, that accurate information about sexual assault can greatly reduce a person's risk.

The community education program's two objectives were to increase awareness about nonstranger sexual assault and provide information about what people should do if they or someone they know are assaulted. Although this effort had the potential to increase the number of reported sexual assaults (making it appear the problem was increasing), we could not truly manage a crime that was so underreported because of the misconceptions and shame surrounding this type of assault.

SDPD Speaker's Bureau: Content Development

As a result of the meeting and attendees' recommendations, the Sex Crimes Unit developed a Speaker's Bureau to provide education that would reduce sexual assaults in San Diego—with particular emphasis on nonstranger sexual assaults. Volunteers present the Speaker's Bureau curriculum, which includes information on the prevalence of nonstranger sexual assault; the methods offenders use to select and lure their victims; common assault locations, times of day and days of the week; and the influence of drugs and alcohol on the likelihood of sexual assault.

Rather than focusing on traditional self-defense tactics that are often ineffective in cases involving nonstrangers, our curriculum encourages young women to be assertive, establish boundaries and honor their instincts. We also encourage men and boys to support women and girls in being assertive. Primary prevention messages for men and boys include the legal definitions of sexual assault and the criminal consequences of such behavior. Our presentations also include a scenario of attempted sexual assault that stimulates students' discussion of the dynamics of nonstranger sexual assault, including predatory behavior, pressure to participate in sexual activity and assertive responses.

SDPD Speaker's Bureau: The Challenging Road to Implementation

In 1993, a 40-hour Speaker's Bureau Academy trained volunteers to deliver the curriculum. The Speaker's Bureau includes men and women from diverse ethnic backgrounds who range in age from 25 to 65 years.

Because our analysis indicated 75 percent of sexual assault victims who reported to the SDPD were between 14 and 25 years of age, the Speaker's Bureau's original intent was to begin education efforts in middle schools. We found, however, this was not possible in 1993. In fact, the school system initially determined that we could not talk to high school students about their attitudes, values or behaviors without a signed parental consent form for each student. Some school administrators were also seriously concerned that the type of education we proposed would increase reports of sexual assaults, detracting from parents' perception of school safety.

Thankfully, our relationship with the school system resulted in modifications to our presentation. San Diego City Schools in 1995 accepted a 50-minute curriculum for high school students. These presentations, and others to private institutions, have been very well received. As of June 2000, the SDPD has offered 542 presentations to community members, mostly to high school and college students. This represents more than 16,000 individuals who have received this vital information. In 2001, the SDPD Speaker's Bureau received permission to present a curriculum specifically designed for middle school students.

Educating Law Enforcement:
Identifying the Training Need

Once the Speaker's Bureau activities were running smoothly, we began analyzing the data to understand the characteristics of law enforcement's response to nonstranger sexual assault. Perhaps predictably, this analysis revealed another serious problem: Law enforcement personnel had some of the same misunderstandings about sexual assault as the rest of the community. Specifically, investigating officers often equated sexual assault with stranger assault.

Forensic investigations of sexual assault by a stranger are very different from those involving a nonstranger sexual assault. Officers have traditionally been taught to identify biological evidence, latent prints, tire marks, fibers and shoe prints as potential evidence. This evidence is typically used to identify a suspect or confirm a suspect's identity. Sexual assault investigation textbooks and training continue to emphasize the collection of evidence that would ensure identification of a stranger suspect. As an example, both of the roleplaying scenarios used at the San Diego Regional Police Academy involved stranger suspects and weapons. A review of the State of California curriculum also revealed that sample case scenarios illustrated the investigation of stranger assaults.

As a result of this training, we found officers looked for serious injury, weapons and immediate cries for help to establish the elements of force or fear and to judge the victim's credibility. Officers tended to question the victim's story if weapons were not present or if he or she failed to report the crime quickly, not recognizing that only a small percentage of reported sexual assaults actually involve weapons and that delayed reporting is not uncommon in nonstranger sexual assault.

Obviously, identification is not the primary investigative issue in nonstranger sexual assault. The suspect in such crimes frequently admits the sexual encounter took place, claiming it was consensual. The challenge to investigators of these crimes is the collection and identification of evidence that demonstrates lack of consent. Unfortunately, sexual assault investigators trained with the image of a stranger assailant all too often collect evidence geared toward identification—missing opportunities to collect, describe or emphasize the very necessary evidence supporting lack of consent. Officers and prosecutors must be trained to look for subtle pieces of evidence that will help corroborate the victim's account. These can include any sign of a struggle, such as a knocked-over plant, a spilled glass, stretched elastic on a pair of panties or a missing button from a blouse.

Implementing Training

After identifying this significant training need, the SDPD Sex Crimes Unit made major modifications to the Regional Police Academy's curriculum to address the investigation of nonstranger sexual assault and establish lack of consent. Scenarios were modified at the state and local level, and Rape Crisis Center advocates were included as academy staff to ensure the scenarios were accurate and law enforcement responses appropriate. In addition to the basic academy classes, the Sex Crimes Unit developed 40 hours of advanced training for officers and detectives that includes such topics as investigating crimes of sexual assault, sex crime laws, designer drug identification, drug-facilitated sexual assault, forensics, victim interviews, and impact and community resources.

STUDY OF SEXUAL ASSAULTS REPORTED TO THE SDPD, 1994–96

The Unit's analysis of reported sex crimes continues annually; we now have nine full years of data. In 1996, we enlisted the help of an epidemiologist at San Diego State University's Graduate School of Public Health to provide more in-depth analysis. Of particular interest was how the context and character of a sexual assault affected the case's legal outcome. The study sought primarily to describe reported sexual assaults for a three-year period and identify factors most strongly associated with successfully charging and prosecuting an identified suspect. Information was collected from police logs and records, as well as evidentiary examinations performed at local hospitals. We will first describe the character and context of the sexual assaults in the study sample, then outline the law enforcement outcomes.

Study Sample

The study examined all reported sexual assault cases from 1994 through 1996 involving the crimes of rape, marital rape, sodomy and penetration with a foreign object (n=1,228 cases) (Lindsay 1998). Only cases involving a female victim and one or more male suspects were included; cases describing the crimes of attempted rape, oral copulation, sexual battery, incest and unlawful sexual intercourse with a minor (statutory rape) were excluded. (Unlawful sexual intercourse with a minor does not have the elements of force, duress and menace that characterize the penal code classification of rape.) Cases involving the rape of a minor (adolescents), however, were included.

Victim Age and Relationship to Suspect

As stated above, all the victims in the study were female. Overall, 76 percent of cases involved an adult victim, and 24 percent were adolescents (14 to 17 years). In 27 percent of cases, the victim described the suspect as a stranger; the remaining 73 percent were nonstranger cases. These nonstranger cases were further divided into two categories: "brief encounter" and "acquaintance" cases. A brief encounter case (13% of all 1,228 cases) was defined as a case in which the victim knew the suspect for less than 24 hours. These cases were analyzed separately because they differ strongly from acquaintance cases. From the victim's perspective, for example, the assailant was essentially a stranger because she had spent only limited time with him at a bar, party or other gathering prior to the assault. Yet from the perspective of law enforcement investigators, these brief encounter cases were often seen as acquaintance cases because the victim and suspect spent time together prior to the assault.

Data from this study clarify the common misconception that nonstranger sexual assault is equivalent to date rape. Among the nonstranger cases (n=894) in our sample, only 19 percent involved dating relationships. The majority of nonstranger cases involved nondating relationships (57%) that included neighbors, friends of friends, friends of boyfriends, co-workers, etc.

Location

Figure 2 describes the location of the assault in terms of the victim's relationship to the suspect. Stranger assaults most often occurred outdoors or in a car (59%). Conversely, the majority of acquaintance assaults occurred in either the victim's home (40%) or the suspect's home (33%), indicating some level of trust between the victim and suspect prior to the assault. The majority of brief encounter assaults occurred either in the suspect's home (35%) or outdoors/in a car (30%). The location category of "indoor" in Figure 2 refers most often to parties or the homes of friends the victim and suspect were visiting.

Length of Time from Assault to Police Report

Figure 3 (see page 34) describes the length of time from the assault to the filing of a police report. The length of time from assault to report has important implications for investigators' ability to obtain an accurate history of events and important crime scene evidence, as well as for the victim to receive a timely forensic examination. Overall, 64 percent of cases were reported within 72 hours; however, women reporting assaults by strangers were much more likely to report the crime earlier than women reporting assaults by acquaintances. The length of time from assault to report for brief encounters falls between the other two categories. In addition to making the cases harder to investigate, delays in reporting acquaintance cases may influence perception of the victim's believability by those investigating the allegations and/or judges and jurors if the case goes to trial.

Weapons

The stereotypical image of a sexual assault often involves a stranger who uses some form of weapon. Our data refutes this prevailing belief, showing that such weapons as knives, guns or broken bottles were used in only 15 percent of cases. Figure 4 (see page 35) describes the suspect's use of a weapon in both adolescent and adult victim cases by relationship to the suspect category. Weapons were involved much less frequently in adolescent cases than in adult cases. Weapons were used more frequently in stranger assaults than

Figure 2. Location of Assault

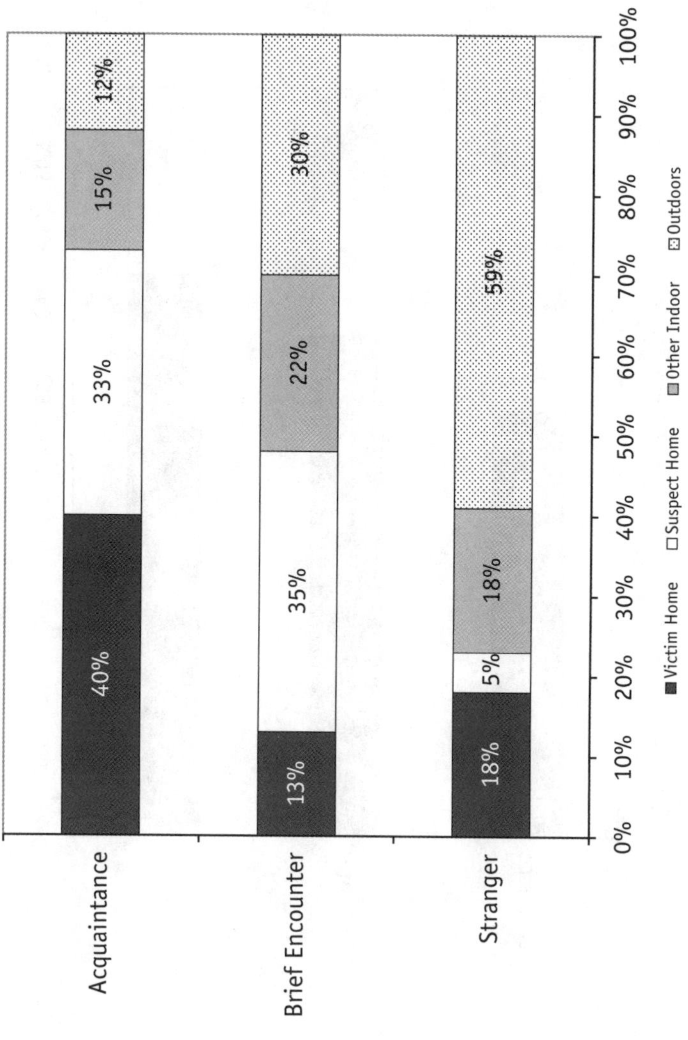

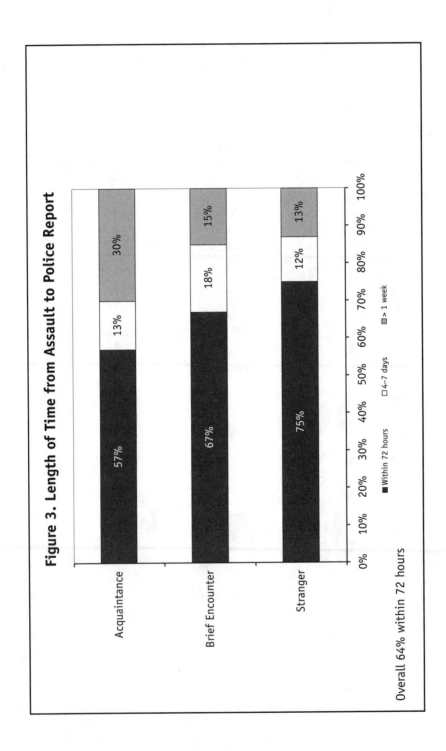

Figure 3. Length of Time from Assault to Police Report

Overall 64% within 72 hours

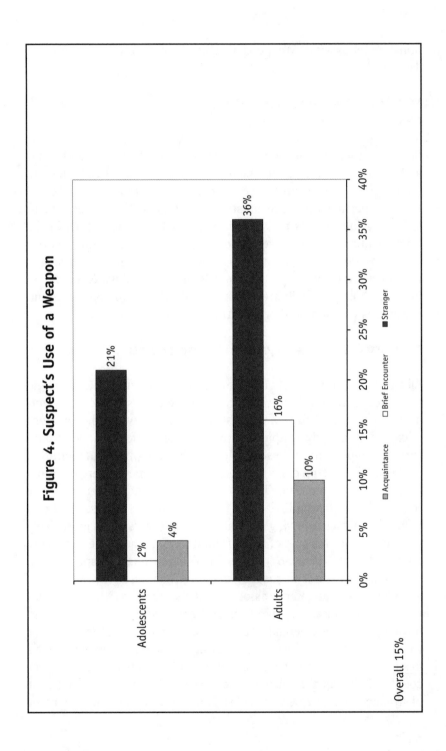

Figure 4. Suspect's Use of a Weapon

■ Acquaintance   □ Brief Encounter   ■ Stranger

Overall 15%

nonstranger assaults. Weapons were used only rarely in acquaintance assaults.

Victim's Self-Reported Use of Drugs and/or Alcohol

Figure 5 describes the victim's self-reported, voluntary use of drugs and/or alcohol prior to the assault. This figure dramatically demonstrates the relationship between drug and alcohol use and sexual assault—particularly in the nonstranger category. Thirty-four percent (34%) of adult victims and 53 percent of adolescent victims in the brief encounter category self-reported drug and/or alcohol use prior to the assaults; they were thus particularly susceptible to assailants who exploited both their trust and their vulnerability. Not only do drugs and alcohol facilitate sexual assault, they also contribute uncertainties to attempted prosecution.

Criminal Justice System Responses

All the factors described above combine to influence the investigation, prosecution and judicial outcome of sexual assault cases. Overall, the San Diego Office of the District Attorney reviewed 41 percent of cases in the study sample for possible prosecution of an identified suspect; 40 percent of these resulted in the charging of an identified suspect. Adult victim cases with nonstranger suspects were the most frequently reported crime in the study sample and were most likely to be reviewed by the DA's office (primarily because the suspect was identified). Cases involving adolescent victims were much more likely to result in the charging of an identified suspect than cases involving adult victims (55% vs. 36%). Cases involving stranger suspects were more likely to result in suspect charging than cases involving brief encounter or acquaintance assailants (60% stranger, 41% brief encounter, 37% acquaintance). Significant differences in suspect charging, however, exist between adult and adolescent victim cases. For adult victim cases, those involving an identified stranger assailant were the most likely to result in suspect charging (65% stranger, 30% brief encounter, 32% acquaintance). For adolescent victim cases, 44 percent of stranger cases, 62 percent of brief encounter cases and 54 percent

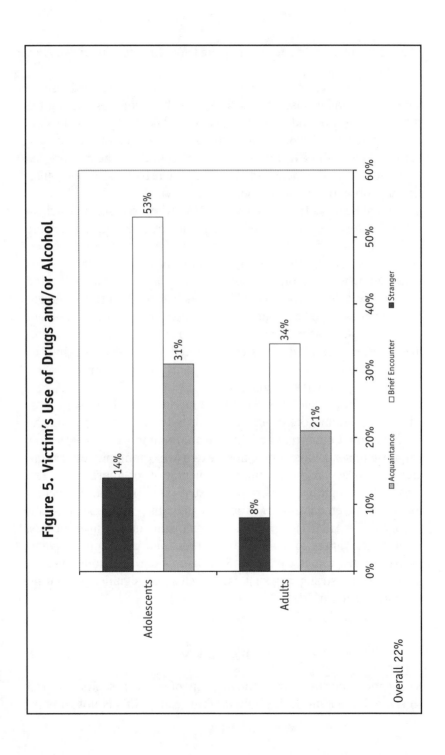

Figure 5. Victim's Use of Drugs and/or Alcohol

of acquaintance cases reviewed by the DA's office resulted in suspect charging.

It is interesting to note that the percentage of DA-reviewed cases in which an identified suspect was charged with a crime rose during the three-year study period, from 30 percent in 1994 to 39 percent in 1995 and 53 percent in 1996. Although the percentage of suspects charged increased for all three relationship categories, much of the increase can be attributed to the increased charging of nonstranger suspects (particularly those in the brief encounter category).

Figure 6 shows the percentage of DA-reviewed cases in which an identified suspect was charged with a crime by year and relationship of victim to suspect. In 1994, 40 percent of stranger cases, 23 percent of brief encounter cases and 30 percent of acquaintance cases reviewed by the DA's office resulted in the charging of an identified suspect. By 1996, suspect charging rates had climbed to 67 percent of stranger cases, 64 percent of brief encounter cases and 48 percent of acquaintance cases. Note the tremendous increase in the percentage of brief encounter cases that resulted in suspect charging. By 1996, brief encounter suspects were being charged almost as frequently as identified stranger suspects.

In a retrospective observational study such as this, it is not possible to determine the exact causes for a dramatic shift during the study period. Concurrent activities related to improving San Diego's response to sexual assault included extensive community education, victim advocacy activities, the implementation of improved strategies for investigating nonstranger sexual assaults and the development and implementation of an active, community-wide Sexual Assault Response Team (SART)—including law enforcement, victim advocates, forensic examiners, public health workers and prosecutors. Whatever the causes, it is clear that San Diego's understanding and response to nonstranger sexual assault changed significantly during the three-year period.

SUMMARY

Strangers do not perpetrate the majority of sexual assaults reported to law enforcement in the United States today. This is not to mini-

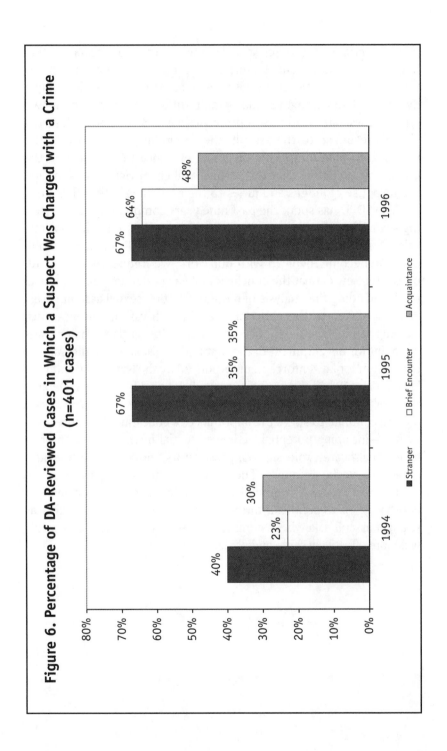

Figure 6. Percentage of DA-Reviewed Cases in Which a Suspect Was Charged with a Crime (n=401 cases)

mize the crime of stranger sexual assault; rather to emphasize that our beliefs about sexual assault, our response to sexual assault victims and our investigative strategies need to recognize the unique dynamics of nonstranger sexual assault. Differences between the two types of assaults include the prior victim/suspect relationship, the victim's response to the assault, the community's response to the victim, the value of specific pieces of evidence in establishing the crime, the likelihood that the suspect will claim victim consent and the response of judges and juries to the nonstranger sexual assault.

The SDPD has spent the past nine years comprehensively analyzing sexual assaults reported to its Sex Crimes Unit and will continue this effort. Each year, more organizations and individual stakeholders have become involved with our work; we frequently receive requests for new data at the conclusion of each calendar year. Our local work (including the analysis of more than 5,000 sexual assault cases) has been taken to the national level through various publications, training seminars and national conferences. It was also a major starting point for development of the first national sexual assault training curriculum for law enforcement, produced by the National Center for Women and Policing through a grant sponsored by the U.S. Department of Justice.

We continue to stress the importance of educating the entire community—including potential victims, potential offenders, law enforcement, healthcare professionals, prosecutors, judges and future jury pools—about the dynamics of nonstranger sexual assault. By doing so, we hope to create a community that understands rape involving a nonstranger is as serious a threat to community health and safety as stranger assault. Likewise, a criminal justice system that recognizes this will more effectively serve and protect its community.

References

Arata, C., and B. Burkhart. 1996. Post-Traumatic Stress Disorder Among College Student Victims of Acquaintance Assault. In *Sexual Coercion in Dating Relationships,* S. Byers and L. O'Sullivan, eds. New York: The Haworth Press.

Bachman, R., and L. E. Saltzman. 1995. *National Crime Victimization Survey.* Violence Against Women: Estimates from the Redesigned Survey. Washington, D.C.: U.S. Department of Justice, Bureau of Justice Statistics. Available online at http://ojp.usdoj.gov/bjs/abstract/femvied.htm.

Burgess, A. W., ed. 1985. *Rape and Sexual Assault: A Research Handbook.* New York: Garland Publishing.

Fairstein, L. 1993. *Sexual Violence: Our War Against Rape.* New York: Berkley Books.

Galvin, J. 1985. Rape: A Decade of Reform. *Crime and Delinquency* 31(2):163–68.

Gidycz, C., and M. Koss. 1991. The Effects of Acquaintance Rape on the Female Victim. In *Acquaintance Rape: The Hidden Crime,* A. Parrot and L. Bechhofer, eds. New York: John Wiley and Sons.

Greenfeld, L. 1997. Sex Offenses and Offenders: An Analysis of Data on Rape and Sexual Assault. U.S. Department of Justice, Bureau of Justice Statistics. Available online at http://ojp.usdoj.gov/bjs/abstract/soo.htm.

Katz, B. 1991. The Psychological Impact of Stranger Versus Nonstranger Rape on Victims' Recovery. In *Acquaintance Rape: The Hidden Crime,* A. Parrot and L. Bechhofer, eds. New York: John Wiley and Sons.

LeBeau, J. 1988. Statute Revision and the Reporting of Rape. *Sociology and Social Research* 72(3):201–7.

Lindsay, S. 1998. An Epidemiologic Study of the Influence of Victim Age and Relationship to the Suspect on the Results of Evidentiary Examinations and Law Enforcement Outcomes in Cases of Reported Sexual Assault. Doctoral dissertation. University of California at San Diego.

Marsh, J. 1988. What Have We Learned About Legislative Remedies for Rape? *Annals of the New York Academy of Sciences* 528:388–99.

Parrot, A., and L. Bechhofer, eds. 1991. *Acquaintance Rape: The Hidden Crime.* New York: John Wiley and Sons.

Spears, J., and C. Spohn. 1997. The Effects of Evidence Factors and
    Victim Characteristics on Prosecutors Charging Decisions in Sexual
    Assault Cases. *Justice Quarterly* 14(3):501–24.

POLICE RESPONSE TO PEOPLE WITH MENTAL ILLNESS

Sheldon F. Greenberg

> Because of failings in the community care system, po-
> lice have been thrust into the frontline. They are the
> only service which can be relied upon to get to a scene
> within minutes and can be called out 24 hours a day.
> —*National Schizophrenia Fellowship (BBC 1999)*

Mental illness is not a lifestyle or a choice; it is a medical disease. Scientific consensus holds that major mental illnesses—notably schizophrenia, manic-depressive psychosis and clinical depression—are brain
diseases and, like other diseases, can be treated (Isaac and Jaffe 1996).
To this day, however, community-based treatment has not received the
support necessary to realize its potential, and a large segment of the
population remains without service or with limited service. To put this
in perspective, an estimated 4.5 million Americans have the severest
forms of serious brain disorders: schizophrenia (2.2 million people) and
bipolar disorder (2.3 million people). The National Advisory Mental Health
Council estimates that on any given day, 40 percent of these individuals
(1.8 million people) do not receive treatment (Torrey 1995).

People with mental illness are frequently caught up in the criminal justice system because of the way their illnesses manifest when
untreated. While even the best response and intervention by police
cannot cure this population, police agencies are making progress interacting with them and their families. Some police agencies—such
as Milwaukee, Wisc.; Memphis, Tenn.; Los Angeles, Calif.; Montgomery County, Md.; Ft. Lauderdale, Fla.; and Madison, Wisc.—have significantly changed the way they serve people with mental illness.
These agencies work closely with mental health providers, support
mental health response teams and designate officers to cooperate

with the mental health community. Yet the majority of police agencies and officers nationwide respond to calls involving people with mental illness the same way they have for decades. As of the late 1990s, of 194 cities in the United States with populations of 100,000 or more, only 78 had a special program for dealing with the mentally ill (Deane et al. 1999). Among smaller and medium-size agencies, the percentage with programs or access to services is much smaller.

One challenge for police agencies wishing to reform their responses is resolving the mixed messages officers receive from executives, trainers, supervisors, politicians and the community. Officers hear about the need to problem solve and take the time to bring lasting resolution to calls for service; they also hear about the need to pursue hospitalization rather than criminalization for people with mental illness. At the same time, they are told not to generate overtime or engage in activities that pull them from the road for extended periods. They learn that the vast majority of people with mental illness never become violent; at the same time, they hear about officers injured when interacting with the mentally ill and that people with mental illness commit "something like 1,000 homicides" each year. Perplexed officers must then sort out these issues themselves because too few agencies bring order to this complex topic.

This chapter discusses the problem for police and identifies ways agencies can change their policies and practices to improve the situation for all involved. The following section explores the nature of the problem by describing the transition of responsibility from the mental health system to the criminal justice system, where roles and traditional responses complicate the response to people with mental illness. The second section details methods of addressing the problem, including improved police responses, protocols and education.

THE NATURE OF THE PROBLEM

Responsibility Shift

That police officers will respond to calls for service involving people with mental illness is certain; how often and with what consequences, however, is not well known.[1] This is because only a handful of police agencies keep accurate information. There is no mandate to maintain precise records about calls for service involving people with mental illness, and many argue doing so would violate certain rights of those with disabilities. Yet this lack of accurate information inhibits change and fosters prevailing misperceptions.

Nevertheless, some national data do describe the nature of the problem for police. In the National Institute of Justice's National Assessment Program survey, for example, chiefs of police, sheriffs and jail administrators cited a shift in the way people with mental illness are served by the criminal justice system (McEwen 1995). This shift reflects public expectations that police involvement will go beyond report taking, incarceration and emergency hospitalization to include

- more in-depth involvement and intervention,
- family support,
- diffusing of crises,
- rapid and quality referrals, and
- teaming with mental health practitioners.

The chiefs and sheriffs acknowledged that although calls for service related to mental illness occur at a relatively lower rate than other types of calls, they are increasing in frequency. In addition, the complexity of the calls—in which people with different types of mental illness have different needs—presents difficulties that result in lengthy police involvement (McEwen 1995).

Cities that maintain information on calls involving people with mental illness provide further information on the trends. In New York, for example, calls for service for "emotionally disturbed persons" have increased yearly since the early 1980s, from 20,843 in 1980 to 46,845 in 1988 and 64,424 in 1998 (Bumiller 1999). A study of California sheriffs' departments revealed that incidents involving people with mental illness increased to 9 percent of all emergency calls for service—up from 3 percent five years prior (Husted, Charter and Perrou 1995). In less than one year, the Tampa Police Department responded to more than 3,400

---

[1] This chapter focuses on those cases in which mental illness is a factor in the incident.

emergency calls involving people with mental illness and people threatening suicide (of approximately 32,000 calls for service).

The Memphis Police Department began collecting data in 1987,
after police killed a man in a public housing complex who threatened
suicide. Since that time, police contacts with people with mental illness have increased 97 percent (Carlton 1997). Similar increases have
been recorded by the St. Louis Police Department: The number of
people taken to hospitals for emergency evaluation has risen, as have
repeat calls to the same residence. In a 60-day period, St. Louis officers responded to one home 48 times to deal with a person who has
mental illness (Carlton 1997).

As a consequence of their increased involvement, police have become a primary access to the mental health system for people with
mental illness. At the St. Louis Metropolitan Psychiatric Center, one
of the nation's largest, police generate 53 percent of all emergency
room admissions. Police involvement has done little, though, to provide long-term solutions. Doctors at the Center admit there is a re-
volving door pattern in which people are stabilized, medicated and
released. That person will often then fail to take medication, and the
process begins again.

There are many reasons for the increase in calls for service. Mass
deinstitutionalization during the 1960s and 1970s overburdened the
already strained community, mental health system and police resources. Many people with mental illness were left to fend for themselves when the government's goal of large-scale community-based
treatment and support services was not realized. This was com-
pounded by the lack of research and scientific study on how to rein-
troduce people with severe psychiatric illness to the community. There
was no time or priority given to gearing up, developing police policy
or improving officers' skills to serve the expanded, community-based
population of people with mental illness.

Despite the frequency of calls for service involving people with
mental illness, most justice agencies are ill-equipped to respond effectively (McDonald and Teitelbaum 1994). Traditional approaches to
resolving calls for service have not worked for people with mental
illness and, in many cases, have resulted in negative and costly consequences for both citizens and officers. The difficulty with traditional responses relates directly to the complexity of the police role.

Complexity of the Police Role

Although the police role in nonthreatening calls involving people with mental illness is fairly clear, their role in crises or threatening situations is more complex. Family members, complainants, witnesses and others expect police in a crisis to be social workers, crisis counselors, ministers and sages. Few people at the scene realize the police are first and foremost officers of the law. They must make judgments based on safety, law, policy, caring, extent of the threat and more. The police must deal with the situation as police, employing force when necessary (Tollson 1999). Every effort should be made to deescalate the situation. Still, the overall safety of citizens and officers is paramount and must prevail, despite concerns over second-guessing and possible litigation.

Further complicating matters is the misperception many police officers (like much of the general population) have of the degree to which violence and mental illness are linked. This misperception is often based on media reports and anecdotes that do not reflect a complete understanding. American Psychiatric Association research suggests only a small subgroup of people with severe and persistent mental illness are at risk of becoming violent; it is far more likely a person with mental illness will be the victim of violence and other forms of abuse rather than the perpetrator (APA 1994). These data, while important to understanding the scope of mental illness, do not negate the serious attention needed when responding effectively to calls involving those people whose mental illness is a factor in an incident and who have the potential to become violent.

Traditional Police Responses

Police respond to a wide range of issues involving people with mental illness, including public safety concerns, the need for crisis resolution, a lack of immediate access to mental health services and the commission of minor offenses (such as loitering and public nuisance). In addition, police often encounter people with mental illness who are victims of theft, assault, harassment or family abuse. Calls for service also continue to be generated by people who are uncomfortable or do not know how to deal with mental illness. The mere presence of a person with mental illness acting out causes them to seek police assistance, even though the individual's actions cause no harm.

In many cases, police officers may arrest the person for minor offenses—a practice referred to as "criminalizing the mentally ill"—because they know the mental health system cannot provide needed or timely support. These "mercy bookings" occur when police seek to protect people with the severest forms of psychiatric illness. This is particularly common when the person in need is homeless and highly vulnerable to victimization. The officer knows the person needs to be removed from the street and takes the most expedient route to facilitate shelter—arrest or placement in a lock-up facility.

Not all cases in which officers criminalize the situation are meritorious. Too often, arrest is simply expedient. This happens when officers do not want to spend the time required to get an individual placed in a treatment facility or wrangle with the process of emergency commitment or hospitalization. It happens when businesspeople pressure the police for a rapid resolution to a situation in which people with mental illness act out and disturb customers. It happens when families, in frustration, implore the police to arrest because they are fearful or feel that is the most expedient way to obtain needed support.

In situations where a person with mental illness is the victim of a crime, police too often assume the victimization is a consequence of the mental illness or the person's current situation (such as homelessness) or is a co-occurring disorder (such as alcohol or other substance abuse). With these perceptions, officers may not respond as diligently as they would to a person who is well. This disparity in treatment can worsen the already considerable resistance to reporting victimization felt by people with mental illness. In one study, only 51 percent of adult victims of traumatic crime who had a diagnosed psychiatric disorder reported their victimization to police (Marley and Buila 1999). The frequency with which victimization is reported drops further if the person with mental illness resides in a group home, has a history of substance abuse, is diagnosed with schizophrenia or is victimized by an authority figure or someone close to them (Marley and Buila 1999).

Consequences for the Criminal Justice System

Despite some agencies' efforts to avoid criminalizing people with mental illness, their presence in jails, lock-ups and other correctional facilities continues to rise. According to a 1998 Department of Justice survey, 16 percent of the total population in the nation's jails and prisons has serious mental illness (Ditton 1999). This is more than four times the total number of people in state hospitals for the mentally ill (Bureau of Justice Statistics 1996). Jails have become surrogate mental hospitals (Torrey et al. 1992).

The frequency of mental illness among youths involved in the juvenile justice system also has increased. The prevalence of mental health disorders among young people in the general population is unclear, and research in this area is lacking. It has been estimated, however, that at least one in five young people in the juvenile justice system has a serious mental health problem (Cocozza and Skowyra 2000).

Once in the criminal justice system, a person's access to needed mental health services diminishes significantly. Most medical insurance and federal programs supporting those in community mental health facilities are not available to people in prison (Schmitt 1999). And the cost is excessive when the criminal justice system is tasked with providing for and overseeing people with mental illness who are in jail for minor offenses. Incarcerating people with mental illness costs more than twice as much as providing support in community treatment programs—$135 per day versus $60 per day (Treatment Advocacy Center 2000).

ADDRESSING THE PROBLEM

Many changes can improve police response to calls involving people with mental illness. While there is legitimate need for such resources as increased beds, co-occurring disorder treatment, 24-hour mental health system support and greater access to qualified medical professionals, much needed change can sometimes simply require greater focus on policy-related matters and attention to basic human dignity. The following sections describe a wide range of ways police agencies can change their response practices, communication protocols and education.

Early Innovative Police Responses

Milwaukee, 1978: The Wisconsin Correctional Service (WCS), a private, nonprofit agency, takes a lead role in supporting people with mental illness who come into contact with the criminal justice system. WCS sponsors the Community Support Program (CSP), which addresses medical and therapeutic services, money management, housing, daily reporting and monitoring, and participation of mentally ill offenders in the community. (Generally, WCS clients have had problems with police because of behaviors resulting from insufficient treatment.) Once engaged in the program, many people comply willingly because they receive substantial benefits, needed social services and life supports. Some even choose to stay in the program for years, well beyond cessation of their legal obligation.

By the mid-1990s, CSP had grown and was providing service to 200 clients each day. The program's elements can be adapted quite readily to other jurisdictions, and CSP has since been replicated throughout the Milwaukee region.

In 1983, New Orleans established a mental health mobile crisis response service, sponsored by the New Orleans Police Department and the state's mental health services. Unlike teams in other cities that consist of mental health professionals or police officers, the New Orleans teams comprise highly trained volunteers. These volunteers are not sworn officers, but they receive a limited commission empowering them to place individuals in mental health facilities when needed. Besides significantly reducing the amount of time officers spend on follow-up support to people with mental illness, the volunteer team program diverts individuals from the criminal justice system to the mental health system. It has been estimated that the teams improve service to people with mental illness, save New Orleans about $300,000 per year and have played a role in reducing the number of suits brought against police by people with mental illness and their advocates (Wellborn 1999).

Recent Innovations in Police Response

Variations on these and other approaches have been gaining across the country in recent years. The most well known and frequently replicated approach is that used by the Memphis, Tennessee, police department. This approach uses Crisis Intervention Teams (CIT) composed of squads of officers specially trained to provide direct support at the scene and who have unlimited access to psychiatric emergency room treatment. The program has been cited as a significant contributor in reducing the number of injuries to both people with mental illness and officers. While calls involving people with mental illness have doubled in Memphis during the past ten years, the number of officers injured has dropped by more than 75 percent (Gettleman and Wexler 1998).

Memphis's success has led to similar programs nationwide, including those in Washington, D.C.; Montgomery County, Md.; and Albuquerque, N.M. The Montgomery County program builds on the Memphis model but was modified to meet the county's strengths, such as a longstanding collaboration between police and mental health service providers. As in Memphis, the Montgomery County program is based on officers who volunteer to serve on crisis intervention teams. Volunteerism is, in fact, at the heart of these programs' success. The officers are educated and certified to provide direct service, including one-on-one communication and on-site assessment, to people with mental illness and their families. Officers receive no incentive pay or other remuneration but are allowed to wear a team insignia on their uniform. The success of the program in Montgomery County has resulted in a waiting list of volunteers, as well as reduced liability and improved response to other types of calls for service (Hill and Logan 2001).

In Madison, Wisconsin, the police department played a lead role in establishing the Program of Assertive Community Treatment (PACT), another approach gaining popularity. PACT provides multidisciplinary services to people with mental illness 24 hours per day. In addition, the Madison police department assigned one sergeant half-time to liaise between the department and the region's mental health agencies.

Ft. Lauderdale, Florida, established a mental health court to address cases involving misdemeanors committed by people with mental illness. The court considers the offenders' special needs and the circumstances that may have influenced their behavior. The court does not neglect criminal wrongdoing or seek to give an "easy out" to people who clearly had malicious intent. It acts to prevent unnecessarily criminalization of people with mental illness while recognizing that others may have been victimized.

Language and Communication Protocols

Many police agencies "dehumanize" people with mental illness, beginning with the initial call for service. For example, the basic "10 Code" references a 10-96 as "mental subject" (APCO 2000). Many agencies, large and small, use codes based on derogatory slang to dispatch calls involving people with mental illness. One large east coast agency that considers itself progressive uses the code MO, for "mentally off"; another uses NC, for "nut case." In a large west coast city, officers are dispatched to calls for MDPs, or mentally disordered persons. These are longstanding, accepted practices that undermine efforts to respond compassionately.

Given the complexity of calls for service involving people with mental illness—and the potential trauma to all people involved—there is little place for humor, brevity or stripping of dignity. The language used in the initial call for service sets the tone for all that may follow. Positive change can begin with simple shifts in vernacular, as well as a commitment by the agency and, particularly, supervisors to reinforce the change. Humanizing or professionalizing the initial call for service by referring to the situation as one involving "a person with mental illness" costs nothing and puts little or no strain on the system.

Another area for improvement is the quality of information communicated by dispatch to the responding officer. Few police communications centers rely on an established protocol—a series of specific questions that must be answered and mandated procedures—to gather data for officers responding to calls involving people with mental illness. Officers therefore tend to respond with far less information than is available and necessary to provide appropriate resolution. Effectively used, however, dispatch protocols and quality communications procedures can improve officer safety and minimize unnecessary escalation.

Dispatch protocols should provide officers with information about the individual's characteristics (particularly if he or she is acting out), the nature of any medication taken, family members, contacts, prior incidents, exposure to potential weapons, behavior in the hours prior to acting out and much more. When quality protocols are in place, responding officers can focus their thoughts on the approach, resources to involve and other issues rather than speculating about the environment they are about to enter and what the individual is doing.

Educating the Police

For more than 15 years, since passage of the Americans with Disabilities Act and publication of a model training curriculum by the Police Executive Research Forum and the Department of Justice, increased emphasis has been placed on delivering quality education to police personnel by leaders in law enforcement and the mental health community (Murphy 1984). Yet progress has been slow. A review of 28 police academy curricula revealed the average amount of training provided to recruits on the subject of police response to people with mental illness is less than four hours (Police Executive Leadership Program 2000). The length of the instructional programs ranged from two to eight hours, with only one of the 28 agencies providing eight hours.

The bulk of the training provided to entry-level recruits focuses on the forms and processes associated with emergency hospitalization or commitment; the remainder of the training addresses violent or potentially violent encounters. Instruction on the characteristics of various forms of mental illness and how to interact with family members was minimal.

In-service training in these agencies ranges from zero to eight hours and generally deals with the same topics (Police Executive Leadership Program 2000). Of the 28 academy programs studied, only 17 required in-service instruction on people with mental illness for all officers. In the remaining 11 agencies, training was optional or provided to a select group of officers. Of the 28 curricula, 10 provided specific guidance to officers on the importance of and ways to support family members. Family members or representatives of mental health agencies were presenters in 12 of the 28 instructional programs. While most curricula appeared to be based on straight lecture, 13 allocated time for class discussion.

The most common reason given for not allowing more time to educate police about calls involving people with mental illness is lack of time—an age-old concern. Training directors are compelled (or feel compelled) to move officers out of the classroom and back to their assignments without spending more time than is absolutely necessary on education, regardless of the complexity or importance of the topic.

There are exceptions to the "rushed training" approach. Among numerous police departments that have taken a leap forward in improving education and training and, subsequently, serving people with mental illness is Baltimore County, Maryland. This department was among the first in the nation to commit to a 40-hour in-service training program, currently offered at least once each year. It is open to both Baltimore County personnel and those of other jurisdictions.

The Baltimore County curriculum opens with a police officer who has personal experience with mental illness telling his or her story. As officers in the audience begin connecting the issue to a peer, the course immediately takes on a personal dimension. Students spend an extensive amount of time with experts from the mental health community, people with mental illness, family members and others. For a period of the program, officers are put into a situation in which they experience some of the fears, confusion and dilemmas faced by people with mental illness. The program allows for extensive discussion and debate over operational issues, time demands, support resources and officer safety. Similar programs—such as the 40-hour program sponsored by the Oxnard, California, Police Department—are providing officers with new understanding and techniques for intervention and de-escalation.

CONCLUSIONS

Positive change is occurring nationwide as more police and mental health agencies recognize the inadequacy of traditional approaches to responding to people with mental illness. While the number of agencies creating alternatives remains relatively small, their programs are being duplicated with increased frequency.

There are some core principles for improving care for people with mental illness who have come into contact with the criminal justice system (particularly the police). Among these principles are improved education for police on mental illness and mental health, coordinated services for those in need, integrated treatment and response for those with co-occurring disorders (for example, mental illness and substance abuse), aftercare for those released from hospitals and jails, and a single point of contact for police and others who need access to mental health services, particularly in a crisis (Lurigio 2000).[2]

Police leaders need to rethink their agencies' policies and practices to incorporate these principles. It is no longer sufficient to have a policy that simply addresses procedures for involuntary placement or commitment. Policies need to be expanded to address such issues as the officer's role in prevention, definitions and measurement of dangerousness, and interaction with mental health professionals for purposes other than commitment (Faenza et al. 1999).

Dr. Gary Cordner of Eastern Kentucky University suggests that police should take a community policing approach to people with mental illness. He notes that such an approach has the potential to reduce use-of-force tragedies while improving overall service; patrol officers assigned to neighborhoods become more directly involved in collaboration, partnerships, prevention and problem solving. Currently, patrol officers react and process calls for service based on the partnerships and steps taken by executives. Cordner calls for beat officers to visit people with mental illness who are likely to experience mental health emergencies, as well as their families, to enhance prevention and intervention. Such visits will require attention, since they could be perceived as intrusive if not carefully handled. Many are worried about the stigma associated with having a police officer visit the home. While visitation may not work in every community, a more proactive, community policing approach to working with people with mental illness, their families, and mental health providers and advocates does offer promise (Cordner 2000).

The community policing approach suggested by Cordner and others goes beyond simply changing policy, meeting with mental health providers or expanding instruction to a recruit or in-service class. Rather, it involves changing the culture of policing to recognize and

---

[2] The Council of State Governments—a nonprofit, nonpartisan organization— has partnered with the Police Executive Research Forum (PERF), Pretrial Services Resource Center (PSRC), the Association of State Correctional Administrators (ASCA) and the National Association of State Mental Health Program Directors (NASMHPD) to prepare these recommendations.

accept people with mental illness as a population justifiably and understandably in need of service. Some agencies have succeeded in modifying that culture, but long-term, sustained change is needed nationwide. This is the challenge for police leaders, mental health providers, advocacy groups, and people with mental illness and their families.

REFERENCES

American Psychiatric Association (APA). 1994. *Fact Sheet: Violence and Mental Illness.* Washington, D.C.: American Psychiatric Association.

Association of Public-Safety Communications Officials International (APCO). 2000. *APCO Radio Code of the Anne Arundel County (MD) Police Department.* Daytona Beach, Fla.: APCO.

British Broadcasting Corporation (BBC). 1999. *Report on the March 18, 1999, Meeting of the London Metropolitan Police and the National Schizophrenia Fellowship.* London, England: British Broadcasting Corporation.

Bumiller, E. 1999. In Wake of Attack, Giuliani Cracks Down on Homeless. *New York Times,* 20 November.

Bureau of Justice Statistics. 1996. *Source Book: Criminal Justice Statistics.* Washington, D.C.: U.S. Department of Justice.

Carlton, J. G. 1997. *St. Louis Post-Dispatch,* 21 April.

Cocozza, J., and K. Skowyra. 2000. Youth with Mental Health Disorders: Issues and Emerging Responses. *Juvenile Justice* 7(1):3–11.

Cordner, G. 2000. Community Policing Approach to Persons with Mental Illness. *Journal of the American Academy of Psychiatry and the Law* 28(3):326–31.

Deane, M., H. Steadman, R. Borum, B. Veysey and J. Morrissey. 1999. Emerging Partnerships Between Mental Health and Law Enforcement. *Psychiatric Services* 50(1):99–101.

Ditton, P. M. 1999. *Mental Health and Treatment of Inmates and Probationers.* Washington, D.C.: U.S. Department of Justice.

Faenza, M., R. W. Glover, G. P. Hutchings and J. A. Radack. 1999. *Mental Illness and the Myth of Violence.* Thousand Oaks, Calif.: Sage Publications.

Gettleman, J., and K. Wexler. 1998. Police Look at Policy on Mentally Ill. *St. Petersburg Times,* 22 November.

Hill, R., and J. Logan. 2001. Civil Liability and Mental Illness: A Proactive Model to Mitigate Claims. *The Police Chief* 68(6):29–32.

Husted, J. R., R. A. Charter and B. Perrou. 1995. California Law Enforcement Agencies and the Mentally Ill Offender. *Journal of the American Academy of Psychiatry and the Law* 23(3):315–29.

Isaac, J., and D. Jaffe. 1996. Toward Rational Commitment Laws. *National Review,* January 29: 34, 36, 38.

Lurigio, A. 2000. Persons with Serious Mental Illness in the Criminal Justice System: Background, Prevalence, and Principles of Care. *Criminal Justice Policy Review* 11(4):312–28.

Marley, J., and S. Buila. 1999. When Violence Happens to People with Mental Illness: Disclosing Victimization. *American Journal of Orthopsychiatry* 69(3):398–402.

McDonald, D., and M. Teitelbaum. 1994. *Managing Mentally Ill Offenders in the Community: Milwaukee's Community Support Program.* Washington, D.C.: National Institute of Justice.

McEwen, T. 1995. *National Assessment Program: 1994 Survey Results.* Washington, D.C.: National Institute of Justice.

Murphy, G. 1984. *Managing Persons with Mental Illness: A Curriculum Guide for Trainers.* Washington, D.C.: Police Executive Research Forum.

Police Executive Leadership Program. 2000. *Review of Police Academy Curricula.* Unpublished manuscript. Johns Hopkins University, Baltimore, Maryland.

Schmitt, S. 1999. Criminalizing the Mentally Ill. *Counseling Today* (October).

Tollson, M. 1999. Tense Encounters, Tragic Consequences. *The Houston Chronicle, Star Edition,* 6 September.

Torrey, E. F. 1995. *Violence: Unfortunate and All Too Often Tragic Side Effect of Untreated Severe Mental Illness.* Arlington, Va: Treatment Advocacy Center.

Torrey, E. F., J. Stieber, J. Ezekiel, S. M. Wolfe, J. Sharfstein, J. H. Noble and L. M. Flynn. 1992. *Criminalizing the Seriously Mentally Ill.* Washington, D.C.: Public Citizens Health Research Group.

Treatment Advocacy Center. 2000. *Criminalization of Americans with Severe Psychiatric Illnesses.* Arlington, Va.: Treatment Advocacy Center.

Wellborn, J. 1999. Responding to Individuals with Mental Illness. *FBI Law Enforcement Bulletin* 68(11):6–8.

4

RESPONDING TO RACIALLY BIASED POLICING THROUGH COLLABORATIVE PROBLEM SOLVING

Lorie A. Fridell

The vast majority of law enforcement officers—of all ranks, nationwide—are dedicated men and women committed to serving all citizens with fairness and dignity. They do not tolerate racially biased policing and are seeking ways to detect and eradicate it in partnerships with citizens. Developing remedies for racially biased policing in concert with concerned citizens may be as important as the remedies themselves. Collaborative problem solving provides one vehicle for this effort. Collaboration fosters residents' trust in police, brings a fresh perspective to the issues and increases the credibility of—and receptivity to—responses. Through shared effort, police and citizens identify and analyze the issues, then develop joint responses and assess their effectiveness.

This chapter proposes a process for applying the problem-solving model to racially biased policing. It represents just one part of ongoing efforts by the Police Executive Research Forum (PERF) to address this important problem. Some other efforts mentioned in this chapter include our report *Racially Biased Policing: A Principled Response*[1] (Fridell et al. 2001) and our work in Lowell, Mass., and Chicago, Ill.

NATURE OF THE PROBLEM

In its poll of December 1999, The Gallup Organization found a majority of both whites and blacks (56 percent of whites and 77 percent of

---

[1] Some material in this chapter is excerpted from the report, which is available in its entirety on the PERF Website (http://www.policeforum.org).

blacks)[2] believed "racial profiling" to be widespread. The practice was defined as "police officers stopping motorists of certain racial or ethnic groups because the officers believe that these groups are more likely than others to commit certain types of crimes" (The Gallup Organization 1999).

More recently, Gallup found that 44 percent of blacks believe "police have stopped them at some time in their life because of their race or ethnic background." Only 7 percent of white respondents and 29 percent of Hispanic respondents felt this way (The Gallup Organization 2001).

Though the term "racial profiling" is modern, the problem it labels has been a part of policing for many years. Today's issue is the latest manifestation of a long history of sometimes tense, and even volatile, police-minority relations. In early discussions, "racial profiling" was defined as police enforcement actions based *solely* on race. Several years of recent attention to this problem have led to an expanded notion of the issue and a move away from the narrow term (see, e.g., Davis 2001; Ramirez, McDevitt and Farrell 2000). The PERF report, for instance, adopts the term "racially biased policing," which occurs "when law enforcement inappropriately considers race or ethnicity in deciding with whom and how to intervene in an enforcement capacity."[3]

Although, as discussed more thoroughly below, there are great challenges in *measuring* racially biased policing, some studies have produced results of clear racial disparity in law enforcement that require serious attention to the issue. John Lamberth (1994), for instance, collected data on drivers stopped by police on the New Jersey Turnpike. He found that while only 14 percent of cars on the roadway had a black occupant—and only 15 percent of cars exceeding the speed limit had black occupants—a full 44 percent of drivers stopped by police in one particular road segment were black.

---

[2]No data were provided for other races/ethnicities.

[3]Chapter 4 of the PERF report articulates more precisely what this means through a proposed policy.

Similarly compelling were the findings of the *Orlando Sentinel*, which analyzed in-car videotapes of 1,100 police stops conducted in Volusia County, Fla. The paper found that, while blacks and Hispanics constituted only about 5 percent of drivers on a particular stretch of I-95, they accounted for more than 70 percent of drivers stopped by police. The videotapes also showed minorities were stopped for longer periods of time than whites and that 80 percent of the people searched were minorities (Brazil and Berry 1992; Curtis 1992).

Police are now looking to the public for partnerships and collaborative problem-solving solutions to a variety of community ills. If substantial segments of the community are the victims of police bias, or even *perceive* they are, success is not likely unless police seriously commit to partnering with the community to address these issues. The following section describes how departments can work with residents—minority and nonminority—to address the serious problem of racially biased policing.

USING COLLABORATIVE PROBLEM SOLVING: ENGAGING THE COMMUNITY

At a neighborhood or jurisdiction level, the issues surrounding racially biased policing can be addressed effectively through collaborative problem solving. This model emphasizes community involvement in identifying problems and their solutions. Involving the community can be valuable for many—if not most—problem-solving efforts and is particularly important for addressing racially biased policing, which divides police and community and threatens trust. Addressing the problem in concert with concerned citizens not only brings in fresh ideas and perspectives, but serves as a mechanism for building trust. Citizen involvement also adds credibility to the department's efforts and implies a shared responsibility for resolving the issues.

One way to engage the community is by developing a police-citizen task force dedicated to addressing racially biased policing. A jurisdiction-wide task force could advise the agency executive, but police personnel might also develop neighborhood-based task forces to focus on specific geographic areas.

The jurisdiction-wide task force should comprise 15 to 25 people representing both the department and community. In selecting community members, emphasis should be given to those most concerned with police racial bias. The task force also should include representatives from the jurisdiction's various minority groups, as well as civil rights groups. Police personnel selected should represent all levels of the department, including patrol. Diverse viewpoints should be represented, and a representative from the police union should participate, if applicable. A neighborhood task force should be similar, with concerned citizens and patrol officers participating.

The police departments in Lowell, Mass., and Chicago, Ill., have successfully initiated discussions with their communities about racially biased policing. In Lowell, one focus group that convened for the PERF project on racially biased policing has been transformed into a police-citizen task force. Citizens and police officers met initially to discuss racially biased policing, particularly during vehicle stops. After some finger-pointing, raised voices, citizen accusations and defensiveness on both sides, the group began developing ways to resolve the identified problems. Without prompting from the facilitator, participants agreed they needed to meet regularly to continue sharing, listening and resolving problems.

The chief has continued the group as the Race Relations Council. They have met a number of times and have come up with new ideas regarding police-citizen communication and police training (including a video they will produce on cultural diversity and a new police-citizen cross-training curriculum). The Council also is planning a community-wide survey with questions on racial bias and experiences with police.

Chicago's work to address police racial bias and perceptions of its practice is based on solid police-citizen collaboration. At the outset, Chicago's police superintendent sponsored a series of forums for police and minority community residents. PERF invited community activists and department staff of all ranks to participate. Before the first forum, participants answered a survey on their opinions about racially biased policing, the department's strengths and weaknesses regarding minority outreach, and how to improve police-minority relations and resolve issues.

An independent facilitator (PERF Executive Director Chuck Wexler) moderated the initial sessions. During the first forum, community members shared their thoughts, experiences and concerns in the morning, while police staff listened and held their responses until later in the day. In the afternoon, police staff shared their thoughts and reactions to the morning session; this time, citizens were instructed to listen and not respond. During the final session of the day, all participants joined in a discussion of the issues and ideas raised earlier. Subsequent, ongoing discussions have identified specific actions both police and community members can take.

Terminology is important and should be discussed at the first gathering of any police-resident group addressing racially biased policing or "racial profiling." When conducting focus groups around the country with citizens and police practitioners, PERF project staff discovered the term "racial profiling" hindered discussion. Most *citizens* used the term "racial profiling" to discuss all manifestations of racial bias in policing. The *police* participants were likely to define "racial profiling" quite narrowly——as law enforcement activities (particularly vehicle stops) based *solely* on race. The citizens claimed that "racial profiling," as they defined it, was widespread. In contrast, the police (using their more narrow definition) were frequently adamant that police activities based solely on race were quite rare. These contrasting, but unspoken, definitions led to police defensiveness and citizen frustration.

We found that citizens and police can have constructive conversation on the topic of "racially biased policing" (or such similarly broad phrases as "bias-based policing"[4]). These terms more accurately reflect the citizens' concerns, and few police would deny that some officers are influenced by personal bias in performing their duties, whatever the motivation.

Jurisdiction- or neighborhood-wide groups should agree on a definition of the problem their collaboration addresses.

---

[4]This terminology was adopted by the National Organization of Black Law Enforcement Executives, or NOBLE (see Davis 2001).

COLLABORATIVE PROBLEM SOLVING: APPLYING THE SARA MODEL TO RACIALLY BIASED POLICING

Collaborating community members and police should follow the SARA (Scanning, Analysis, Response and Assessment) problem-solving model. This process involves clear identification of a problem, investigation of the problem using various sources of information, development of tailored responses and evaluation of those responses' effectiveness. This section describes how the SARA model might be applied to racially biased policing, perceptions of its practice and the racially disparate impact of law enforcement activities.

Scanning

In scanning, the police-citizen task force at the jurisdiction- or neighborhood-level would attempt to identify the nature of the problem(s). The ultimate goal of scanning is to identify the who, what, when and where of problems. It is possible this process will identify several and varied aspects of racially biased policing or the perceptions of its practice that must be prioritized to ensure the group is not overwhelmed.

Methods for scanning the issues related to racially biased policing include (but are not limited to) community surveys, focus groups, interviews and review of department data.

Community surveys. Surveys of residents can identify manifestations of racially biased policing or police actions that promote perceptions of racially biased policing. (Our inability in some instances to determine whether the manifestation is *real* or *perceived* need not deter us; the task force should address both, even if they cannot be fully disentangled.) A survey of residents might solicit

- overall attitudes toward the police department,
- perceptions of whether police treat people differently based on race/ethnicity and
- perceptions regarding the circumstances of differential treatment.

Further, such surveys might help determine the extent to which police contact various racial/ethnic groups and in what circumstances. To uncover possible disparate police engagement of minorities, a North Carolina team in 1998 surveyed residents about the nature (e.g., speed, passing behavior, driving violations), location (e.g., interstate highway) and amount of their driving (Zingraff et al. 2000). Additional questions solicited information on the frequency and nature of their encounters with police. Respondents reported how many times they had been pulled over by police and provided information about the most recent incidents (e.g., perceived reason for the stop, disposition, officer actions/demeanor). The survey aimed in part to explore the feasibility of this method for assessing whether law enforcement actions appear to target minorities disparately when (self-reported) driving quantity and behavior are held constant.

Similarly, the Bureau of Justice Statistics (BJS) recently added questions to the National Crime Victimization Survey regarding police-public contacts.[5] Key questions from this survey that jurisdictions might use to compare their data to the national results produced by BJS include

- whether the respondent has had face-to-face contact with police in the last 12 months;
- the respondent's perception of the reason for the face-to-face interaction with police;
- whether the respondent was questioned, ticketed, arrested and/or searched during the encounter;
- the respondent's perception of the legitimacy of any search; and
- whether physical force was used or threatened.

Focus groups. A great value of focus groups with residents is that they allow citizens to vent their anger and frustrations. That is, while these forums can be used to collect scanning information, they also can be part of the healing process. Facilitators should *expect* raised voices and finger-pointing and consider these as healthy aspects of

---

[5] A copy of the Police Public Contact Survey is available on the BJS Website (http://www.ojp.usdoj.gov/bjs).

the process. The police-citizen task force can serve as its own focus group, but a jurisdiction also would be well served by holding multiple focus groups with different residents to obtain breadth of input.

Focus groups should comprise 12 to 15 persons and an experienced facilitator who is unaffiliated with the department.[6] Discussion questions should focus on the who, what, where and when of racially biased policing and perceptions of its practice. Similar to the survey options described above, questions might include

- *Do police* treat all residents in the same manner regardless of race or ethnicity?
- If not, *whom* do they treat differently?
- *Under what circumstances* (e.g., during what types of procedures) are people treated differently?
- *How* are they treated differently?

Interviews. One-on-one interviews with residents can be used to solicit the same type of information as the community surveys and focus groups. Though interviews require more labor than surveys or focus groups, they allow more in-depth probing of issues than a survey and provide a context for more frank communications than a group setting. As some residents will not wish to share their thoughts on this topic with sworn agency police, the task force should arrange for civilians to conduct interviews.

Collecting data on the race/ethnicity of residents contacted by police. Despite some claims to the contrary, racially biased policing is not particularly amenable to empirical analysis. As discussed more fully in the PERF report, data collection strategies—that is, collecting data on the race of citizens with whom police engage—are limited by constraints associated with their valid analysis/interpretation. Ideally, data on racially biased policing would indicate where it occurs, who commits it, against whom it is committed, what procedures are most vulnerable to its practice and so forth. In practice, the lack of appro-

---

[6] Local colleges or universities can be good sources of facilitation expertise. An agency might contact departments of psychology, sociology, criminal justice or social work to inquire about assistance.

priate benchmarks limits our ability to disentangle racial bias from other explanations for identified disparity.

Agencies that choose or are required to collect data could, nonetheless, address racial disparities in their data regardless of hypothesized cause. That is, departmental data could be used to scan for racial disparity—but that disparity should not be *presumed* to reflect racial bias on the part of law enforcement officers.

Consider a hypothetical project conducted by the fictitious Northern Police Department that reflects this expanded focus (this example is inspired by work conducted in Seattle). In concert with other agencies and citizens, this department uses data on the race of individuals receiving citations to determine if racial disparities exist. A racial breakdown of traffic infractions and criminal citations, for instance, indicates a large percentage of citations for non–moving violations (e.g., driving with a suspended license and driving without insurance) are given to black drivers. Thus, for instance, while blacks account for only 13 percent of speeding citations, they account for a full 44 percent of citations for driving with a suspended license (see Figure 1, next page). We pick up on this example again in the section on Analysis.

Scanning results. In addition to discoveries like those of the Northern Police Department, the scanning process might produce findings such as the following:

- Minority residents in focus groups perceive they are targeted for traffic stops because of their race/ethnicity.
- Young minority males perceive they are disproportionately targeted for investigative stops they believe are unjustified.
- In focus groups, minority residents report they feel estranged from and not served by the agency.
- Minority residents in a particular neighborhood complain about two particular officers who they believe target young black males for detention and search.

Analysis

While scanning attempts to identify the who, what, when, where and how of identified problems, the key to analysis is collecting informa-

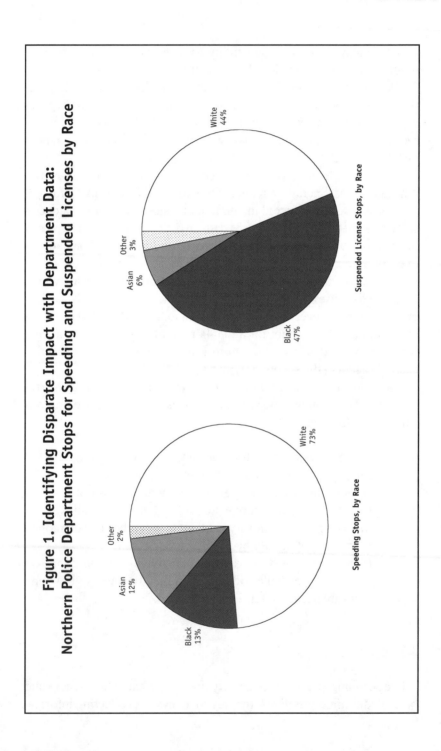

Figure 1. Identifying Disparate Impact with Department Data:
Northern Police Department Stops for Speeding and Suspended Licenses by Race

tion on the question "why?" Analysis is arguably the most important stage of the SARA process because it can produce the information necessary to tailor appropriate and effective responses.

Again, discussions with residents may assist in the analysis of the problem. In fact, facilitators may probe results from scanning focus groups to gather information for analysis. If this preliminary analysis produces information that helps the agency fully understand the issue, additional focus groups may not be necessary. On the other hand, the department may decide to hold additional discussions with residents or select groups of residents (e.g., young minority males) to gather additional information.

The focus groups PERF held with community members produced some information that helped staff understand stated problems. During those focus groups, for instance, a number of minority citizens stated they were being pulled over on traffic stops because of their race/ethnicity. With probing by the facilitator, a number of minorities reported they are likely to interpret negative aspects of a vehicle stop as racially biased policing. For instance, these participants acknowledged that officer rudeness, discourtesy and/or unwillingness to give the reason for a stop might well be perceived as the result of racial bias (as opposed to an overall and impartially demonstrated lack of professionalism, perceived danger by the police officer, etc.).

In talking to minority residents, departments may also find their feelings of estrangement are linked in part to the department's overwhelming Caucasian composition. In one scenario, residents may state that rogue officers in their neighborhood have been partners for 15 years and work the midnight shift or that all complaints to their sergeant fall on deaf ears. Speaking to young black males, the task force may learn more about the context of frequent investigative stops (e.g., locations, time of day and apparent precipitating circumstances). Discussing how they are treated during these stops may reveal that officers have failed to tell why they are being stopped or that officers disengage in an abrupt manner from encounters producing no evidence of wrongdoing.

Some of the information generated through the citizen focus groups might be communicated to officers in similarly small groups to gather feedback for better understanding the problems identified by residents. These groups must be structured to promote honest reflection and frank discussion. The facilitator should be a person independent of both the agency and the task force. In such a focus group, for instance, officers may be asked about the frequent stops of minority males at certain times and locations (as reported by the minority males). The facilitator should get the officers to reflect on why these stops were made. Information from the officers may very well reveal that appropriate actions were taken. A discussion of the officers' legal rationales for the stops might indicate whether and how race/ethnicity played a part; this in turn might reveal whether officers use racial stereotypes in their decision-making.

An anonymous survey of officers can provide more information to help the task force understand problems raised during scanning. The survey might present scenarios reflecting the investigative stops described by minority males and solicit officer input regarding their cause and information on officer actions. As with the focus groups, facilitators could use responses to gauge officers' criteria for establishing the reasonable suspicion to justify such detentions. As above, this may reveal whether or not some officers use stereotypes about black criminality in making certain law enforcement decisions.

Our hypothetical Northern Police Department and its partners seek to understand the reasons for the disproportionate representation of blacks among people cited for suspended licenses. While not dismissing the possibility of bias, they discover through interviews with personnel at the City Attorney's Office and the Municipal Court that most people have their licenses suspended because of failure to pay traffic fines. Census figures show blacks in the jurisdiction are disproportionately represented in the lower income brackets and thus possibly more likely to have trouble paying fines. The next section describes how this information can be used to tailor a response.

Response

During the response phase, the task force develops measures consistent with the information gathered during analysis. The PERF report guides agencies in their response to racially biased policing and the perception of its practice within six areas:

1) accountability and supervision,
2) antibiased policing policy,

   3) recruitment/hiring,
   4) education/training,
   5) minority community outreach and
   6) data collection.

The approximately 50 recommendations in the report may help task forces develop responses reflecting what they learned during analysis.

The finding that minority residents feel estranged from the police department because racial/ethnic diversity is lacking could lead to a minority recruitment/hiring initiative. As conveyed in the PERF report, diversity in the police ranks is necessary to earn minority trust and demonstrate equity to the public. Where the police force reasonably reflects the community's racial makeup, it promotes a general sense of fairness; where it does not, it invites suspicion and mistrust as to why members of various racial and cultural groups are not willing or able to serve in the police ranks.

This type of response is conducive to a joint police-community response. Besides the necessary efforts of the police department, minority residents (task force members in particular) should be called upon to identify, recruit and support minority applicants.

One scanning example was that young minority males perceive they are disproportionately targeted for investigative stops they feel to be unjustified. In analysis, we speculated focus groups might determine the context of these stops: The young men were rarely told why they were stopped, and officers disengaged in an abrupt manner from encounters producing no evidence of wrongdoing. We further considered police focus groups might confirm many officers provide little information, if any, to persons they stop and do disengage abruptly. This led to a conclusion that some officers appeared to use racial stereotypes regarding black criminality as justification for detentions.

Several responses might be warranted in light of this information. Officers could be told to inform detainees of the reason(s) for detention once safe to do so. They might also be told to disengage more respectfully from encounters producing no evidence of crime, providing the rationale for the stop and possibly an apology—*not for their actions* (which should have been fully justified), but for the inconvenience and embarrassment to the resident. The finding that racial stereotypes may enter into some officers' decision-making calls for a clear policy indicating when it is legally relevant to use race/ ethnicity in law enforcement decisions, as well as comprehensive recruit and in-service training in this policy.[7]

Another scanning example was minority residents' perception that their traffic stops were the result of bias. As found in the PERF focus groups, this perception may be due in part to how officers treat all residents during stops. This should lead to clear standards for professional traffic stops, such as those offered in the PERF report. The standards should include a policy whereby officers introduce themselves upon approaching a detained citizen and state the reason for the stop (unless providing this information will compromise officer or public safety) before asking the driver for license and registration. The department might ask citizens who have been stopped to complete and mail in a brief consumer survey on the quality (good and bad) of their encounter with police. This will provide the agency with an ongoing assessment of residents' perceptions and may enhance officer professionalism. As noted above, it may be difficult to determine through analysis whether real bias exists in traffic enforcement; still, this type of policy and training can address or prevent such circumstances.

To address the rogue officers identified during scanning (described as long-time partners without effective supervision), an agency might consider assignment rotations; methods for effectively selecting, training and monitoring supervisors; and an early warning system to identify potential problem officers.

Recall that the Northern Police Department determined during scanning that blacks were disproportionately cited for suspended licenses. It analyzed the situation and discovered most licenses were suspended because of failure to pay traffic fines. In light of this information, the city develops a program allowing payment plans for unpaid traffic fines and consolidation of fines from multiple courts. The purpose is to reduce the number of people with licenses suspended for unpaid fines; the city expects this program will be particularly beneficial for low-income drivers, many of whom are minority. (Results are presented in the next section, Assessment.)

---

[7] The PERF report contains a model policy that serves this purpose.

It is important to note that while the Northern Police Department acknowledged the difficulty in ascertaining whether racial bias was a factor in the disproportionate citations, it responded proactively to the possibility. The department has adopted an anti–racial bias policy, implemented special training on racially biased policing, held police-community forums to discuss the issue and adopted enhanced accountability procedures. It also is implementing a pilot program that puts video cameras in patrol cars and instituting a more comprehensive information-collection system that goes beyond citations.

Assessment

The assessment phase aims to evaluate responses' effectiveness; it should focus on the original problem identified during scanning. Where resources permit, the agency should collect baseline data prior to implementing responses for comparison. Strategies used during the scanning and assessment stages (e.g., community surveys and focus groups) may provide these baseline data.

A first step in assessment is to confirm the response was implemented as designed. That is, before assessing a response's effectiveness, the task force should determine whether and how the desired response was put into effect. From our examples, the task force would determine, for instance, whether the agency

- adopted a policy on officer behavior and trained all personnel in its contents and application,
- informed officers how they should greet persons stopped for traffic violations and how they should handle investigative stops,
- implemented consumer surveys, and
- instituted a minority hiring recruitment strategy.

The next step would be to identify cost-effective methods for determining whether the responses were effective. The methodologies described for scanning and analysis can be used in this phase as well.

To return to our examples, the task force could conduct a second community survey. This might look for any reduction in the proportion of minority residents who perceive their traffic stops are the result of bias or who believe the agency does not reflect—and thus presumably does not fully serve—the minority community.

If the task force used a scenario-based officer survey during analysis to assess how officers use race/ethnicity in their decision-making, it might repeat the survey after policy adoption and training. Likewise, a task force with great foresight would have implemented consumer surveys before the new procedures for traffic stops to uncover any changes in resident feedback.

A department that documents all investigative detentions could contact selected detainees to verify use of the new procedures and record the detainee's perception of the stop's legitimacy and officers' professionalism. (Again, this data will be more meaningful if such interviews were also conducted prior to implementation.) Of course, such information should not be considered valid evidence of officer wrongdoing or linked directly to actions against officers.

The Northern Police Department and its partners assess the effectiveness of their fine-paying program by looking at citations for the two years following implementation (which we will posit was in 1998). Figure 2 reports the absolute number of citations for driving with a suspended license (DWLS) for three racial groups for 1998, 1999 and 2000; it shows a decline in citations for all three groups, with a particular impact on blacks. Indeed, in looking at the percentage of citations received by blacks across the same three years (see Figure 3, second page following), we find blacks experienced the greatest reduction. Whereas blacks accounted for 47 percent of DWLS citations in 1998, they accounted for only 36 percent of cases in 2000.

Assessment information may indicate a successful response or that the response did not affect the original problem identified during scanning—or something in between. Based on this information, an agency should maintain its response, modify the response or possibly return to an earlier stage of the SARA process. Often, returning to the analysis stage can help assess whether inaccurate on incomplete information led to a poorly suited response.

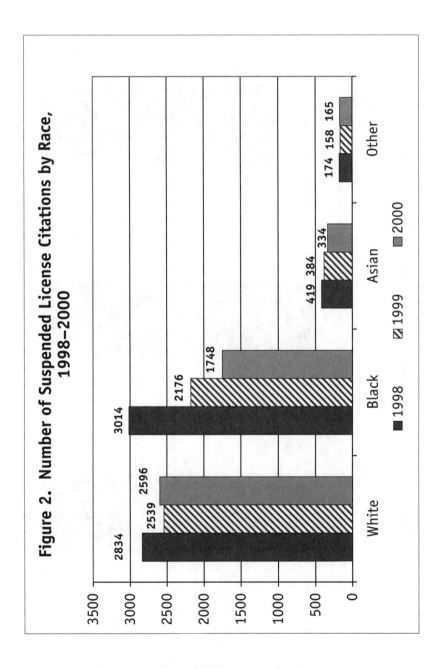

Figure 2. Number of Suspended License Citations by Race, 1998–2000

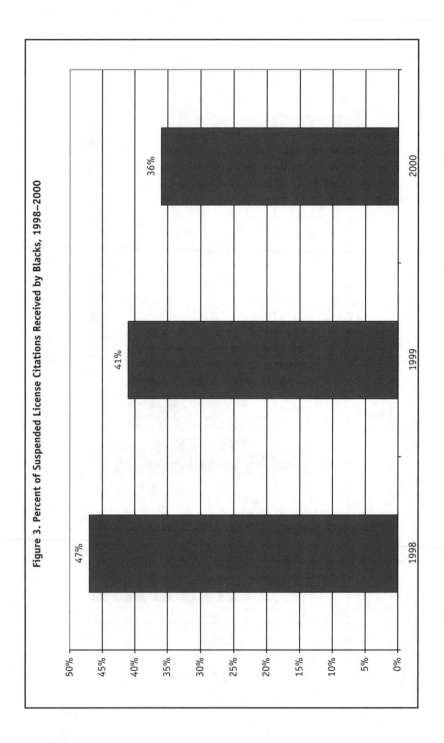

Figure 3. Percent of Suspended License Citations Received by Blacks, 1998–2000

CONCLUSIONS

Racially biased policing presents both a challenge and an opportunity for police to exercise quiet determination and moral leadership. This problem, as much as any, calls for a collaborative effort on the part of police and community. In partnership, police and residents can address this serious problem and practice a method of collaboration that will serve them in future joint efforts.

REFERENCES

Brazil, J., and S. Berry. 1992. Color of Driver Is Key to Stops in I-95 Videos. *Orlando Sentinel,* 23 August, A1.

Curtis, H.P. 1992. Statistics Show Pattern of Discrimination. *Orlando Sentinel,* 23 August, A11.

Davis, R.L. 2001. *A NOBLE Perspective: Racial Profiling—A Symptom of Bias-Based Policing.* Alexandria, Va.: National Organization of Black Law Enforcement Executives.

Fridell, L.A., R. Lunney, D. Diamond and B. Kubu. 2001. *Racially Biased Policing: A Principled Response.* Available online at http://www.policeforum.org. Washington, D.C.: Police Executive Research Forum.

The Gallup Organization. 1999. Racial Profiling Is Seen as Widespread, Particularly Among Young Black Men. Available online at http://www.gallup.com/poll/releases/pr991209.asp.

The Gallup Organization. 2001. Gallup Social Audit on Black/White Relations in the U.S. Available online at http://www.gallup.com/poll/releases/pr010711.asp.

Lamberth, J.L. 1994. Revised Statistical Analysis of the Incidence of Police Stops and Arrests of Black Drivers/Travelers on the New Jersey Turnpike Between Exits or Interchanges 1 and 3 From the Years 1988 through 1991. Unpublished manuscript for Lamberth Consulting.

Ramirez, D., J. McDevitt and A. Farrell. 2000. *A Resource Guide on Racial Profiling Data Collection Systems: Promising Practices and Lessons Learned.* Washington, D.C.: U.S. Department of Justice.

Zingraff, M., H. M. Mason, W. Smith, D. Tomaskovic-Devey, P. Warren, H. L. McMurry and C. R. Fenlon. 2000. Evaluating North Carolina State Highway Patrol Data: Citations, Warnings and Searches in 1998. Report submitted to the North Carolina Department of Crime Control and Public Safety and North Carolina State Highway Patrol, November 1.

5

GRAFFITI PREVENTION AND SUPPRESSION

Corinne Hard, David Tos and Dan Albright

SCANNING:
DEFINING THE GRAFFITI PROBLEM

The San Diego Police Department's Mid-City Division serves a densely populated and ethnically diverse community comprising four square miles of mixed residential and commercial zones. Local schoolchildren speak 38 languages at home, and the population includes both lifelong residents and new immigrants. Housing consists largely of Section 8 (subsidized) apartment complexes. The business district is primarily made up of churches and small family-owned businesses, such as pawnshops, ethnic restaurants, liquor stores, automotive repair shops and thrift stores. The area has long been known for robberies, drug deals, prostitution, auto theft and other street crimes. The police department naturally concentrated on reducing serious crime.

By the late 1990s, the division had already widely adopted problem-solving techniques, including weekly community meetings. At one such meeting in March 1999, an officer presented crime statistics for robberies, prostitution and drug offenses in Mid-City. After listening to the litany, one community member asked, "What about the graffiti problem?" Several others chimed in with, "How are you going to stop graffiti in our neighborhoods?" Residents felt the graffiti was leading to increases in crime—an instance of blight creating blight. The officer was surprised but had to concede that graffiti was an important quality-of-life concern for the community. From that point on, graffiti became a top priority for the Mid-City Division.

A team of two officers and a detective decided to quantify the extent of the graffiti problem. They charted on a map the amount, sites and types of graffiti in the community. After two days of examining two square miles of the division, their findings were staggering: more than 300 instances[1] of pronounced graffiti and nearly 100 instances of graffiti covered over with paint that did not match the original wall color. The community's concern, they realized, was well founded.

ANALYSIS:
UNDERSTANDING THE GRAFFITI PROBLEM

Problems that affect residents' quality of life usually involve many stakeholders. In this case, stakeholders were identified as business owners, merchants, homeowners, local residents, the El Cajon Boulevard Business Improvement Association, shoppers, city government, the school district and the police department.

Through community meetings and contact with officers on the street, the stakeholders communicated their belief that graffiti ranked low on the police department's list of priorities. Community members also expressed concerns that if graffiti continued unchecked, property values would plummet, personal safety would be jeopardized and neighborhoods would decay.

Costs of Countering Graffiti

The team calculated the monetary costs related to countering graffiti and compared them with costs nationwide. In 1998, for example, the San Diego City School District spent $500,000 on paint to cover graffiti. The city spent $24,000 to cover graffiti on walls, curbs and other city property. Additional money was spent on sandblasting, a common method of graffiti removal.

Background and Motives of Taggers

Research disclosed that the demographic profile of graffiti writers (or *taggers*) in Mid-City roughly matched national findings (U.S. Depart-

---

[1] The officers stopped counting at 300.

ment of Justice 1998). One erroneous belief is that taggers come from single-parent homes; a survey of incarcerated local juvenile offenders conducted by Mid-City officers, however, showed 60 percent of taggers were from two-parent households.

The probation department invited 10 convicted taggers to take part in a graffiti focus group. A psychologist counseled the taggers to uncover their motivations. The taggers listed the following reasons for committing acts of vandalism:

- the need for attention and acceptance by peers, parents and teachers;
- the thrill of risk taking;
- the competition against other taggers; and
- the absence of adult role models.

After working with the taggers for three months, the psychologist expanded the reasons mentioned above to include

- lack of intimate adult interaction and direction,
- lack of self-discipline,
- poor self-esteem,
- unresolved life trauma and
- impulsiveness.

In conjunction with the San Diego Association of Governments, the team developed a survey asking juveniles who had been arrested for tagging to explain their motives. Of the 59 juvenile taggers in custody, 25 admitted to tagging. Their motives were boredom, desire for recognition/popularity, gang membership and solo artist recognition.

While exploring the Internet to gain a better understanding of the problem, police discovered numerous Web sites that promote tagging. These sites give taggers a venue to boast about their activity, showcase their work, gain information about the "best" tagging locations in any city and find stores with tagging supplies. (One such site is Graffiti Art by Mear, http://www.mearone.com.)

Graffiti Characteristics

Analysis of the visual survey of graffiti in the division found the following:

- Of the 300 counted instances of graffiti, 265 were concentrated on rented, multifamily housing that bordered business districts; 35 were on single-family houses.
- Business corridors were tagged on many blank walls. The first 30 feet of an alley was also a prime spot because taggers could see if anyone was coming and the tag was visible to passing traffic.
- Alleys, dumpsters, telephone poles, electrical poles and boxes were prime tagging targets because they rarely got painted over.
- School walls were tagged daily.

Crime Statistics

The officers then studied graffiti-related calls-for-service, out-of-service time, the number of graffiti arrests compared with other crime arrests, the most popular times of day for tagging, types of graffiti, the age of suspects and the proximity of tagging to suspects' homes. The San Diego Police Department's Crime Analysis Unit supplied the data. An examination of graffiti-related calls showed the following:

	1998	1999
Calls-for-Service	218 calls	149 calls
Out-of-Service Time	264 hours	227 hours
Arrests	16 arrests	18 arrests

By themselves, these statistics might suggest the graffiti problem was under control. But because of the intense community concern and the fact that the visual survey uncovered more than 300 instances of graffiti, the team concluded the problem was underreported and that there were serious shortfalls in enforcement and arrests. The 300 counted instances of graffiti were concentrated in two square miles of the division, and only 70 percent of graffiti

tags had been reported. Furthermore, police found it difficult to separate graffiti from other instances of vandalism because all vandalism
cases were logged under the same Penal Code Section.

As analysis continued, common aspects of graffiti in Mid-City
began to emerge:

- Graffiti was concentrated near taggers' homes and along
  routes to and from school.
- Tagging was usually a multiple-suspect activity carried out by
  gangs or crews.
- Tagging generally occurred from 5 P.M. to 8 P.M. during the
  week and during all hours on the weekend.
- Tagging by scratching graffiti—with a spark plug on Plexiglas,
  for example—was increasing.
- Graffiti was prevalent near multifamily housing and adjoin-
  ing alleys.

Varieties of Graffiti

The research uncovered three types of tagging in Mid-City: gang, crew
and solo. Gang and crew graffiti mark taggers' home territory and accounted for 90 percent of the graffiti in Mid-City. A tagging crew, each
with its own name, consists of people trying to get into gangs. Both
gangs and crews "bomb in packs"—that is, work as groups to ensure an
extensive attack. Crews often tag directly on top of rival crews' graffiti.
Solo taggers, who account for only 10 percent of the graffiti, are considered lone wolves and attack anywhere to promote their tag names.

The team next identified main sources for each kind of graffiti.
The top two gang graffiti suspects were Oriental Boys Society (OBS)
and Holy Blood Gang (HBG); the top two tagging crew graffiti suspects were Running the Show (RTS) and Van Dyke Krew (VDK). The
top two solo taggers were identified as Clever and Rascal.

Social Aspects of Graffiti

After analyzing the graffiti survey, police examined the social aspects
of graffiti. They found that tagging is part of a natural progression of

acts leading to gang activity. It begins at elementary school with children tagging paper, ball caps and backpacks. The negative behavior is taught in small, intimate settings by people with influence over potential taggers. The research made clear that taggers have a negative social control; that is, taggers lack self-control and are often at the mercy of others who teach criminal behavior. (Kennedy 1998).

Previous and Current Solutions

Police analyzed such past responses to graffiti as surveillance, citizen paint-outs, random patrol, crime reports and arrests, restorative justice, juvenile court, and probation. Though these often had positive effects, none seemed to deter taggers.

One positive approach to deterring criminals is the Pulling Levers theory, which involves advance warning of enforcement, meticulous follow-through and the provision of alternatives to criminal activity (Kennedy 1998). With this in mind, the team looked at successful solutions currently adopted by police departments nationwide to control graffiti.

- **Murals**: Police in Philadelphia and Reno discovered taggers normally leave murals alone because they view murals as art that conveys a sense of ownership. The cities therefore commissioned artists to paint murals around the city to prevent tagging.
- **Colorizing**: A national study found colorized graffiti sites (i.e., those covered with paint the same color as the wall) were 10 times less likely to be retagged. Officers in San Diego, however, found that taggers hit high-visibility sites (such as freeway accesses) on a daily basis, even after colorizing. Alleys were slow to be retagged after colorizing.
- **Counseling**: Counselors in a graffiti-abatement project in Cathedral City, Calif., treated tagging as an addiction. San Diego police endorsed counseling but asserted that tagging is criminal behavior, not an addiction (adapted from National Institute of Justice Office of Community Oriented Policing Services and Police Executive Research Forum 1998).

The team also looked at the national juvenile justice system's methods of dealing with vandalism arrests. Statistics showed that 53 percent of vandalism cases nationwide were handled informally, and 47 percent of those were dismissed (U.S. Department of Justice 1998). In fact, only 28 percent of cases nationwide proceed through the justice system on average. In the Mid-City Division, 75 percent are handled informally, and 25 percent go to formal probation. The team spoke with San Diego juvenile probation officer Carmen Kneile, who said, "We do not have enough case workers to handle the number of juvenile offenders. We need help if we're going to keep on top of the taggers. We carry case loads of up to 100 probationary juveniles at a time."

RESPONSE:
ATTACKING THE GRAFFITI PROBLEM

Based on the in-depth scanning and analysis, officers decided the best problem-solving approach would be to target both active and potential taggers. Youth-oriented resources would have to be the primary partners in this effort, so the police department joined with the community advisory board, youth mentoring programs, city schools, the code compliance-graffiti control program, juvenile probation and the juvenile court. Officers settled on six responses to Mid-City's graffiti problem.

1. **Counseling:** Two social workers volunteered to help. Ten juveniles, chosen for the frequent number of times they were caught tagging, set personal goals to stop tagging. Each week, they met with the counselors to discuss prevention methods; hours counted toward their community service. In the course of the counseling sessions, three juveniles completely stopped tagging (their tags no longer appeared on walls, and police did not catch them tagging). Thus, the counseling group was somewhat effective; due to lack of funding, however, it is no longer implemented.

2. **Paint-outs:** Juveniles on probation for tagging clean up graffiti with bimonthly paint-outs of heavily tagged sites. Police

and juvenile probation, working with Social Advocates for Youth, supervise the paint-outs. Paint and supplies come from the city's Graffiti Control Program, and community members and officers drive around Mid-City to identify tagged areas for colorizing.

3. **Adopt-a-block:** Community stakeholders volunteered to keep a block free of graffiti for six months. The Graffiti Control Program provided paint for the initial colorizing and supplies.

4. **Handler program:** Officers established a list of known chronic taggers by talking to patrol officers and detectives. (The list is secure but accessible to all officers dealing with taggers.) An officer is then assigned to monitor one of these juvenile repeat offenders. The officer, called a "handler," visits weekly with the tagger to monitor his or her behavior. The handler checks on the juvenile's school, home and street contacts and updates the juvenile's file after each visit. A zero-tolerance policy is in effect for repeat offenders; if caught tagging, they are sent back to the probation officer and ordered to perform paint-outs or serve other community service time. The program aims to inform taggers that the community and police department no longer tolerate graffiti. The handler program has greatly assisted juvenile probation with its large caseload.

5. **Murals:** Students at the local junior high school paint murals on heavily tagged walls. The students work with teachers, businesses and residents to plan and to paint murals reflecting positive community images. So far, the students have painted seven murals. Except for some minor pen marks, the murals have escaped tagging.

6. **Joint patrol:** A youth bike team called Kids in Control joined police on bicycles to patrol highly tagged sites. This program improved the relationship between area youth and police officers. Youths were taught to work together to solve crime problems, such as graffiti, in their neighborhood. Officer David Tos wrote a grant for the Mid-City for Youth program to raise money for youth bicycles. Based on the graffiti crime statistics, officers concentrated on youths aged 13 to 18.

ASSESSMENT: GAUGING OUR SUCCESS

A neighborhood inspection 16 months after implementing the responses recorded a 90 percent decrease in tagging. The counseling program had positive results, with 30 percent of taggers in the program curtailing graffiti activity. Unfortunately, the unbudgeted program ended after volunteers finished working with the youths. Juvenile probation continues to work with the police department on paint-outs, assigning 10 juveniles for bimonthly paint-outs in Mid-City. The handler program has 10 chronic graffiti taggers assigned to officers. Police have arrested two of these taggers after visiting their homes; one had drugs in plain view in his room, and the other violated curfew. Police are adding more handlers to the program.

Seven murals have been painted in popular graffiti tagging locations and have remained mostly tag-free. Additional murals are planned. The youths in Kids in Control identified 20 graffiti crews and the neighborhoods in which they tag.

As a result of these new partnerships, graffiti has decreased in Mid-City Division. Efforts and programs will continue to expand, but thanks to their present achievements, San Diego is closer to its goal of removing graffiti from its communities.

REFERENCES

Kennedy, D. 1998. Pulling Levers: Getting Deterrence Right. *National Institute of Justice Journal* 236(1998):2–8 (NCJ 184871).

National Institute of Justice Office of Community Oriented Policing Services and Police Executive Research Forum. 1998. Excellence in Problem-Oriented Policing. *National Institute of Justice Journal* 236 (June).

U.S. Department of Justice. 1998. Juvenile Vandalism. *U.S. Department of Justice—Fact Sheet #85* (October 1998):1.

6

APPLIANCE BURGLARIES[1] FROM RESIDENTIAL CONSTRUCTION SITES

Dan Cunius, Eric Rost and Chuck Johnson

BACKGROUND

Charlie One (C-1) is geographically the largest of the 12 police districts established by the Charlotte-Mecklenburg Police Department (CMPD). Located in the northern portion of Mecklenburg County, C-1 encompasses areas incorporated by the City of Charlotte and the unincorporated areas of Mecklenburg County. (Three smaller municipalities in C-1—the cities of Huntersville, Cornelius and Davidson—each have an independent police department and did not participate in this study.)

Around 1990, the pace of development in northern Mecklenburg county began to accelerate, and the formerly rural area quickly took on a suburban character. Although there was considerable commercial development, especially around the University of North Carolina at Charlotte/Research Park and along some major roadways, the primary growth pattern was single-family residences in subdivisions. During the years of this study (1998–2000), 36 percent of Mecklenburg County's residential growth occurred in C-1 (see Figure 1, next page).

Accompanying this development was a significant rise in burglaries of appliances, building materials and tools from construction sites. C-1 management and officers quickly noticed the increases in reports, complaints, investigator requests and crime statistics. Officers were asked to pay particular attention to construction sites during the night.

---

[1] Appliance Burglary is a break-in to a single-family home under construction that results in an appliance being stolen.

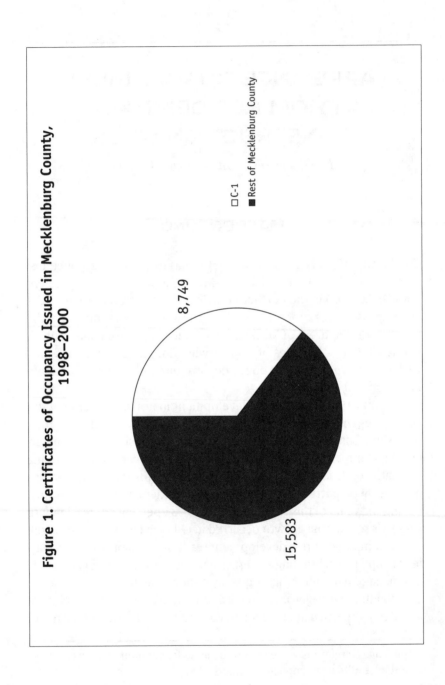

Figure 1. Certificates of Occupancy Issued in Mecklenburg County, 1998–2000

8,749

15,583

□ C-1
■ Rest of Mecklenburg County

But as the pace of construction continued to increase, so did the number of thefts.

In May 1998, C-1 midnight shift officers Dan Cunius and Eric Rost requested dedicated time to work on the construction theft problem from Captain Chuck Johnson. Cunius and Rost suggested directed patrols and stakeouts of construction sites during evenings and nights. They also proposed to work some morning hours to develop contact lists of homebuilders' site supervisors, conduct site security assessments, provide crime prevention ideas to site supervisors and obtain suspect information from investigators to disseminate to third-shift officers. They were willing to change their hours when necessary or work overtime.

EARLY EXPLORATION OF THE PROBLEM

Officers Rost and Cunius contacted construction site supervisors to develop an after-hours contact list and assess security at each site, as well as to let site supervisors know whom in the police department to contact with questions or problems. The contact list had to be abandoned after several months because the construction site supervisors had a high degree of turnover—reassignments and changing employers were the norm.

In assessing site security, Rost and Cunius soon learned the site supervisors knew the subcontractor companies, but not most of the actual employees. (At that time, subcontractors were considered prime suspects.) The officers also found some site supervisors were more aware of security precautions than others. Some site supervisors removed appliance doors to discourage theft and/or used large cargo containers to store tools, materials and appliances. The officers shared this crime prevention information with other builders but recognized that theft prevention measures in any subdivision clearly depended on the site supervisor. The building companies, for the most part, dictated only location, time frame and type of home.

Rost and Cunius also patrolled the construction sites, mostly during evening and nighttime hours. During these patrols, they observed numerous houses containing materials and/or appliances that were left unsecured overnight. In addition, lumber deliveries were not timed to the construction schedules; materials frequently sat for days or over the weekend.

Unfortunately, the directed patrols did not deter thefts. In fact, several times a theft was reported the morning after an evening patrol. Rost and Cunius spoke to officers who worked in an off-duty security capacity for some sites and learned that suspects frequently operated in the early evening hours. Since a host of people visit construction sites at that time—including potential customers, subcontractors and homeowners checking on their builder's progress—suspects are far less likely to be noticed and caught.

EXPLORATION OF THE PROBLEM UNDER CONSULTANTS' GUIDANCE

In 1995, the Charlotte and Mecklenburg County police departments merged to form the Charlotte-Mecklenburg Police Department (CMPD). The Charlotte Police Department had already been moving toward a community-policing philosophy, and new CMPD chief Dennis Nowicki began emphasizing problem solving as the primary unit of work for community policing. As part of his efforts to enhance CMPD's problem-solving capability, Chief Nowicki requested Dr. Herman Goldstein guide selected problem-solving efforts. Goldstein, who developed the problem-oriented policing concept, began working with CMPD in the fall of 1998 under a grant from the Department of Justice's Office of Community-Oriented Policing Services (COPS). Dr. Ron Clarke, who developed the concept of situational crime prevention, joined Goldstein in the spring of 1999.

Goldstein began by examining some of the department's ongoing problem-solving efforts. During this process, Cunius and Rost presented a brief review of their appliance burglary project. After assessing the organization's capabilities and capacities, Goldstein selected the appliance burglary initiative as a suitable candidate for a more ambitious pilot project in February 1999.

The C-1 chain of command (Chief Dennis Nowicki, Deputy Chief Glen Mowrey and Major Norman Garnes) indicated their support for the project, and Captain Johnson assigned Officers Rost and Cunius

full-time to the problem in March 1999. Goldstein and Clarke suggested the officers could accurately portray the scope of the construction theft problem by sharing risk rates with builders. In essence,
a risk rate measures the number of thefts for every 100 homes being
built; this clearly depicts how the problem varies in severity across
geographic regions. To calculate risk rates, the officers had to determine the number of homes being built in C-1 and the rest of the
county, as well as the actual number of thefts.

Rost and Cunius learned 12,000 homes were expected to be built
in the next three years in C-1's 66 subdivisions with ongoing construction (about 2,000 more than official estimates). They next surveyed active builders in C-1 to find out about their security practices;
how they purchased, installed and secured appliances; the brand of
appliances they purchased; their perceptions as to whether appliance theft was a problem; and how they compensated for loss of
appliances.

Survey results indicated that the majority of builders ordered
appliances directly from General Electric (GE); those appliances were
delivered by a company named Contract Express. The other primary
appliance supplier was Whirlpool, which delivered directly to the
house site. In conversations with Contract Express, the officers found
the company was the primary deliverer of appliances to builders, often delivering as many as 100 appliances each day in the Charlotte
region. Contract Express indicated making redeliveries (i.e., replacing stolen appliances) to the majority of builders, with the most frequent redeliveries made to two of the largest builders in the area.

During this time, the officers focused on several suspects identified as being involved in stealing appliances from homes under construction. They received information about possible suspects from
off-duty officers working security, investigators and pawn shop
records. After investigating several open cases in C-1, Rost and Cunius
successfully prepared some cases for the Burglary Unit to present to
the District Attorney's office. Simultaneously, CMPD crime analyst
Carl Walter began mapping subdivisions with residential construction. He also collected data to determine the extent of the construction site theft problem.

In April, Goldstein and Clarke met with the officers, Captain
Johnson and Walter to review the information gathered. During that

conversation, it became apparent construction site theft consisted of three distinct crimes: theft of materials, theft of tools and theft of appliances. The officers convinced the group to narrow the project's scope to appliance thefts because

- there was no way to trace or secure lumber and other materials,
- most subcontractors failed to record the serial numbers of their tools,
- tools were not secured and
- the large and diverse number of subcontractors' personnel made theft prevention education prohibitive.

In contrast, appliances could be traced using their serial numbers, houses at the appliance stage could be secured and builders could disable appliances. Moreover, the team decided to target relatively portable appliances, such as microwaves and clothes washers or dryers, rather than hardwired appliances.[2]

Rost and Cunius also expressed concern with the accuracy of using building permit information to calculate risk rates. Builders often acquired a second permit when the first expired; though that obviously had no affect on the actual risk rate for appliance theft, it significantly distorted calculations using the number of permits to determine the quantity of new homes built. The officers wanted to use Certificates of Occupancy (COs) to judge the amount of building because they were issued only for newly completed homes ready for occupancy. At that time, however, the crime analysis unit was unable to access CO information.

During this meeting, Walter reported his analysis found only 55 appliance burglaries in C-1 during 1998. Clarke expressed concern that the appliance burglary problem was not significant enough to deserve substantial attention (55 burglaries equaled a burglary rate of about one house per hundred built). About a week after the meeting, however, Walter reported a year-to-date total of 28 appliance burglaries through March 1999. Meanwhile, Rost and Cunius collected

---

[2] Hardwired appliances (e.g., cooktops and dishwashers) are wired directly into the building and require inspection prior to issuance of a Certificate of Occupancy.

43 reports from C-1 officers. The ensuing investigation revealed data problems due to errors by reporting officers or by Records Bureau coding clerks. Reports were classified as both Residential and Commercial Burglaries, and appliances were not necessarily being coded into the system as being stolen. Because of this problem, the officers reviewed every C-1 report involving theft from a construction site in 1998. They discovered 109 appliance burglary reports.

After the April meeting, the officers resurveyed builders, this time focusing on the appliance delivery process, installation schedule and post-installation security. They found most appliances were delivered in one installment two to four weeks prior to completion of the home. Builders generally claimed to lock their homes after installation but rarely took any other precautions to prevent theft. (The officers constantly found unsecured homes containing appliances and later documented this in a series of field checks.)

In addition, Rost and Cunius continued to work the suspect angle of the thefts. They contacted GE and Whirlpool, which agreed to check appliance serial numbers to match a particular appliance with a builder and home site destination. The officers then went through pawn records for 1998 and 1999 and had the manufacturers match the serial numbers of appliances that had been pawned. After linking a pawned appliance to a theft report, fingerprint analyses were conducted.

This work linked several suspects with thefts, and several criminal cases were developed. With help from Burglary Investigators, the officers visited auctions and flea markets to identify the destination(s) of stolen appliances. They also gave GE the addresses of burglaries that did not list a serial number for the stolen appliance; GE provided the serial numbers, and the officers added this information to the North Carolina Division of Criminal Information and National Crime Information Center computer systems. The officers also attended bond hearings for suspects of appliance burglaries throughout 1999.

As another tactic to identify and apprehend offenders, the officers recruited neighbors in the newer subdivisions to be informal guardians. They developed a flyer informing new neighbors of theft from construction sites, explaining the problem was countywide and not limited to their neighborhood, and asking them to call the police if they saw suspicious activity. They passed the flyers out door-to-door in some of the newest communities, contacting a number of residents. (The officers tried to convince home builders to pass out flyers, but the builders refused because they did not want people thinking their subdivision had a crime problem.) As a result of passing out the flyers and speaking to residents, the officers located two residents who had seen suspicious activity. These activities were linked to appliance burglaries, and officers successfully prepared two cases.

The problem-solving team met again in August 1999, with crime analyst Ryan Jackson replacing Walter on the project. The officers provided Goldstein and Clarke with a report analyzing appliance theft by such categories as day of week, month, type of appliance, incident per builder for 1998 and 1999, and cost per incident, including loss and repair of damages (see Figure 2 for category of theft). The officers also presented results from their second builders survey.

Discussion centered around the large window of opportunity for theft provided by builders installing appliances as much as a month prior to completing the home. To test whether delaying installation would reduce appliance burglaries, the team decided to develop a presentation for builders based on all the information acquired to date. They hoped to use the presentation to convince builders in one neighborhood to refrain from installing appliances until closing. It was suggested Captain Johnson serve as CMPD spokesman during the presentation to lend the added support of a person of rank.

Shortly after the August 1999 meeting, the officers approached the local Homebuilders Association and found they could obtain actual building permit information for each builder. This information allowed them to clean their data by removing duplicate permits and permits for decks and similar additions. While this new permit information was much more accurate, it still could not account for the skewed appliance burglary rates that resulted from counting building permits.

The officers also approached the Mecklenburg County Engineering and Building Standards Department and learned COs were maintained on a computer database. Not until February 2000, however, were they able to develop a process with Engineering and Building Standards to access CO information.

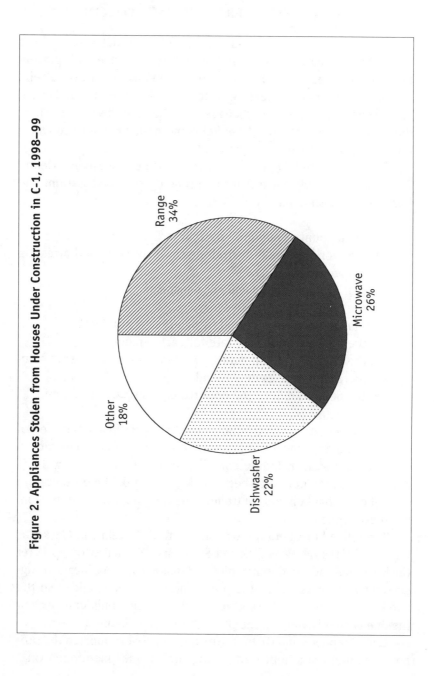

Figure 2. Appliances Stolen from Houses Under Construction in C-1, 1998–99

IMPLEMENTING THE SOLUTION

The officers, crime analyst and Captain Johnson met several times during September to develop and refine the appliance theft presentation for builders. The presentation was then shown to Goldstein, Clarke and others at a meeting near the end of the month. Participants suggested numerous changes, and the team decided to show the presentation to the top 10 builders by volume in C-1 to convince them to delay appliance installation.

Officers Rost and Cunius spent most of the next two months learning to use Microsoft PowerPoint and refining the presentation. The final presentation highlighted

- the amount of building to occur in C-1,
- the work that had been done on identifying and arresting suspects,
- that subcontractors were not suspects,
- the amount of appliance loss,
- that losses were incurred by nearly every builder,
- the appliance burglary rate for each builder,
- the contribution appliance burglaries made to overall commercial burglaries in C-1, and
- the need to reduce the opportunity component of crime.

The presentation asked builders to participate in a trial period of not installing appliances until closing. It also noted CMPD would assess the proposal, including compliance monitoring, during a six-month evaluation period to begin on May 1, 2000. The presentation made it clear that builders controlled offenders' opportunities to commit these crimes.

The refined presentation was shown to Goldstein and Clarke, as well as CMPD's new chief, Darrel Stephens; District Attorney Peter Gilchrist; and the C-1 deputy chief and major. One modification suggested was to personalize the presentation for each builder, so the cited risk rates were not associated with particular builders—except the one currently viewing the presentation (see Figure 3).

Chief Stephens and District Attorney Gilchrist supported the proposed solution and approved having their names mentioned on a

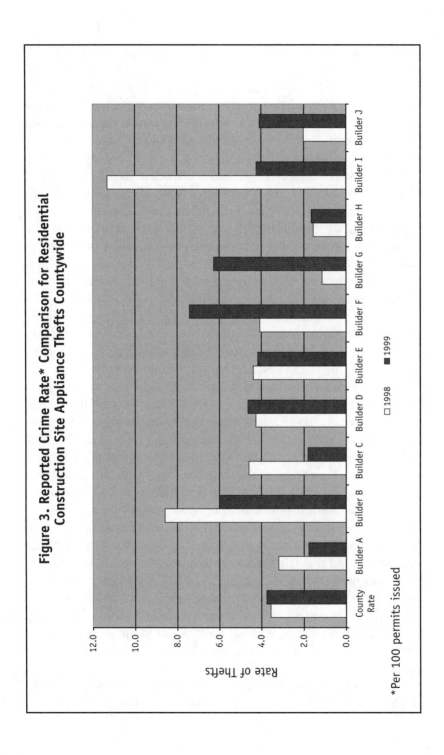

Figure 3. Reported Crime Rate* Comparison for Residential Construction Site Appliance Thefts Countywide

*Per 100 permits issued

supplemental endorsement list. The team also decided to show the presentation to the City Manager's office, the County Manager's office and the City Council's Public Safety Committee to obtain further endorsements that might put subtle pressure on the builders to cooperate. In an attempt to create some peer pressure, the team agreed to add a list that would showcase builders who agreed to support the project.

The presentation was refined and presented to the City and County Managers' offices in December; both endorsed the project. In the meeting with the County Manager's office, the head of the Engineering and Building Standards Department added an endorsement, indicating there was no conflict between delaying installation of appliances and the Building Standards. No presentations were made to builders in December because building is generally slow then, and many people in the industry use this time for vacations.

In January, the officers began contacting the 10 largest builders in C-1 to schedule presentations. Initial contact was with each builder's local home office in an attempt to reach someone high enough in the organization to make a decision on supporting the project.

The first presentation was given to site managers and the sales manager for a company designated here as Builder B. (Builder B had an appliance burglary risk rate above the county average, with a very high ranking in total number of incidents due in part to the high volume of houses it built.) The audience had several questions regarding police knowledge of the suspects in these cases (e.g., whether they were repeat offenders and why they did not stay incarcerated). They also suggested police develop a notice informing potential thieves there were no appliances in a home, to be posted in English and Spanish. The site managers agreed to delay installation of the appliances, and the sales manager indicated he would get this approved by his boss and inform CMPD. In fact, the builder decided to support the project the next morning—but no one called the officers. Only after conducting field checks during May 2000 and seeing that Builder B no longer installed appliances did the officers contact the sales manager and learn Builder B was indeed supporting the project.

The team presented to the City Council's Public Safety Committee in February 2000, picking up another endorsement. The presentation was also shown to the local Homebuilders Association president, but he did not support the project.

During a February meeting with Goldstein and Clarke, the team decided to contact all builders in C-1 because each builder's volume of building varied over time, and some of the larger builders were not cooperative or responsive to repeated police contacts. There also were some ethical concerns about allowing some builders to remain "uninformed victims." The team agreed to show the presentation to CMPD command staff again during the consultants' next visit, to inform them of project details and findings as well as let them know the amount of research conducted.

Over the next four months, Officers Rost and Cunius and Captain Johnson presented to several additional builders. The builders generally had the same questions and concerns regarding the presentation. They wanted to know if CMPD had learned whether the suspects were subcontractors or in the building profession. Several builders expressed concern about the impact of thefts on their sales division and customer perspective. One or two said they could not delay installation until closing but could narrow the gap to the day before closing.

Scheduling and making the presentation was actually quite frustrating. While many builders were responsive and took the time to see the presentation, two never responded to repeated requests for a meeting. Another builder canceled the meeting and never responded further. An additional problem was showing the presentation to someone high enough in the organization to make a decision. After several attempts to get a response from one company, a lower-ranking member of the organization was the only person at the presentation; while this person personally supported the effort, company management did not respond to police contacts. One company agreed to support the project but later retracted; others supported the project, but field checks indicated their compliance rate was poor.

The officers worked on developing a removable sticker reading "Appliances are not in this home" in English and Spanish. They also developed a display placard for use in homes by cooperating builders that said (in English only), "In cooperation with the Charlotte-Mecklenburg Police, appliances will not be installed until occupancy." The team met with Engineering and Building Standards again and finally instituted a means to obtain CO information electronically. This significantly improved everyone's confidence in the refigured appliance burglary risk rates of the district, county and individual builders.

During April, the officers distributed the stickers and display placards to cooperating builders. They also showed the presentation to regional police chiefs and more builders, obtaining additional support from several smaller companies. Lastly, the officers assisted investigators with a case involving a local drug house that served as a fencing operation for stolen goods, including appliances from the construction sites.

TESTING THE EFFECTIVENESS OF DELAYED APPLIANCE INSTALLATION

An April meeting with the consultants helped the team focus on evaluating the new strategy. They decided to conduct field checks of every home under construction in C-1, primarily to measure overall compliance rates and document any differences between participating and nonparticipating builders. The field checks also would help determine the level of appliance burglary underreporting by builders. In addition, the team approached the local newspaper, *The Charlotte Observer*, to gauge its interest in writing an article on the project. (Rob Moore of the *Observer* wrote an article published on April 29, 2000.)

In the meantime, Crime Analyst Ryan consulted with the officers and developed a Microsoft Access database for use in the field checks. The user-friendly database stored a large amount of information with minimal effort and let the officers easily manipulate the data. The time savings also enabled them to conduct many more field checks than would have been possible using a more cumbersome system.

The officers spent the next six months conducting field checks of all homes under construction in C-1—9,753 field checks in all, with 8,050 checks actually involving targeted appliances. On each check, they recorded the security of the house (i.e., if the house could be entered without having to make a forced entry), the presence of any appliances, whether the builder was participating in the project, the presence of a sticker and whether the home was in a preappliance or appliance stage of construction.

After the first two months of field checks, the officers noticed some participating builders had a poor rate of compliance while other nonparticipating builders had a high rate of delayed installation. One small builder not originally contacted (because the company started building after officers' contact efforts) even had a 100 percent compliance rate. With its consent, the builder was added to the list of participants. The officers tracked compliance rates and shared this information with participating builders monthly. They encouraged companies with lower rates to improve and actually met with three companies to discuss their lack of compliance.

ANALYZING THE FIELD CHECK DATA

At the end of October, the officers began analyzing the field check data. Analysis focused on compliance rates, the relationship between risk rates and compliance rates and changes in the overall risk rates for the district and the rest of the county. The purpose was to measure the degree of compliance with the new strategy, the effectiveness of the strategy, the impact on the overall burglary rate within the district and the amount of displacement, if any, to the rest of the CMPD jurisdiction and to nontargeted appliances.

The overall compliance rate for the district was 59 percent. The compliance rate for the 12 participating builders was 78 percent, compared with 43 percent for the 47 nonparticipating builders. Next, the team compared data on the 27 high-compliance builders (those with an overall compliance rate above 50 percent) to data on the 38 builders with an overall compliance rate below 50 percent (see Figure 4, next page). High-compliance builders were issued 965 COs during the six-month test period and had a risk rate of 1.9 appliance burglaries per 100 houses built (the risk rate was 0.8 for target appliances). In contrast, the low-compliance builders were issued 855 COs and had a risk rate of 3.2 for appliance burglary (2.6 for target appliances).

The experience of one company that operated as two separate divisions—one participating and one not—was striking. Company D was the parent company of Company E, which was a participating

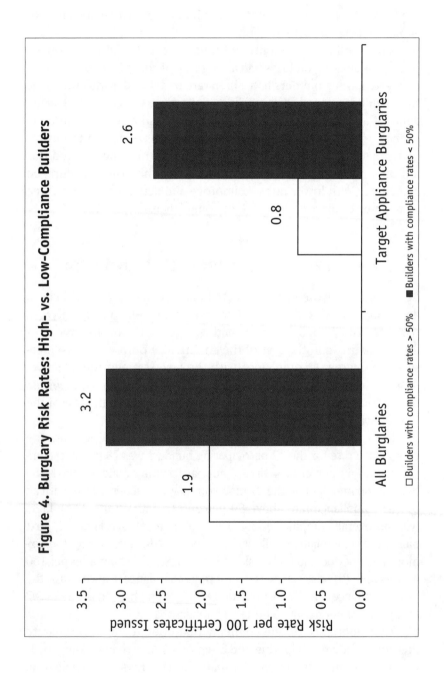

Figure 4. Burglary Risk Rates: High- vs. Low-Compliance Builders

builder with an overall compliance rate of 88 percent. Company D, however, rejected CMPD overtures to participate and had a compliance rate of 8 percent. During the test period, the parent company had a risk rate of 23.1, strongly contrasting with the smaller company's risk rate of 2.8 (see Figure 5, next page).

The team also examined displacement from targeted appliances to hardwired appliances or to homes being built elsewhere in the county. They first compared the gross number of ranges, microwaves, dishwashers and other appliances stolen in C-1 during the same time period for 1998, 1999 and 2000. The number of stolen ranges declined each year. The number of stolen microwaves increased dramatically from 1998 to 1999, but the total 2000 rate of microwave loss was less than the 1998 level. The rate of dishwasher loss was fairly consistent all three years. The loss of other appliances (refrigerators, washers, dryers, etc.) increased significantly from 1998 to 1999, but the rate of loss was lower in 2000 than in 1998 (see Figure 6, second page following). In summary, it does not appear there was any displacement of theft to nontargeted appliances.

The major finding of the study was that during the test period, the overall appliance burglary risk rate for C-1 declined by more than 50 percent compared with the same period of time for 1998 and 1999. The 1998 risk rate (from May 1 to October 31) was 5.4, and the 1999 risk rate 5.3. During the test period, the overall burglary risk rate was 2.5 (see Figure 7, page 108).

Displacement to the rest of the county was tested by comparing the risk rates of the county versus C-1 for May 1 through October 31 for 1998, 1999 and 2000. As mentioned previously, the C-1 risk rate was 5.4 in 1998, 5.3 in 1999 and 2.5 in 2000 (see Figure 7, page 108). The rest of the county's risk rate for the same time periods was 3.0 in 1998, 1.8 in 1999 and 2.2 in 2000. Again, it does not appear there was any displacement of burglaries to the rest of the county (see Figure 8, page 109).

The benefits of delayed appliance installation are illustrated by the decrease in C-1's appliance burglary rate: 4.7 in 1998, 5.6 in 1999 and 3.7 in 2000. Furthermore, during the four months prior to the test period, C-1 had a risk rate of 6.9 and a total of 68 appliance burglaries. Extrapolating a yearly total of appliance burglaries from this rate, C-1 might have experienced 237 appliance burglaries in 2000. Instead there were only 127, with only 58 occurring from May 1 through the end of

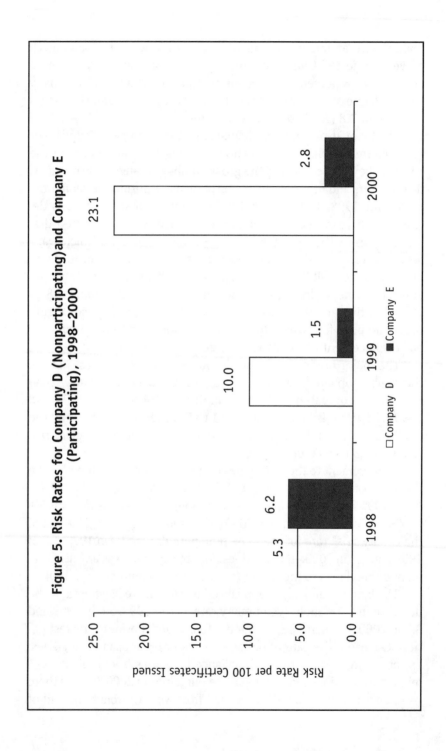

Figure 5. Risk Rates for Company D (Nonparticipating) and Company E (Participating), 1998–2000

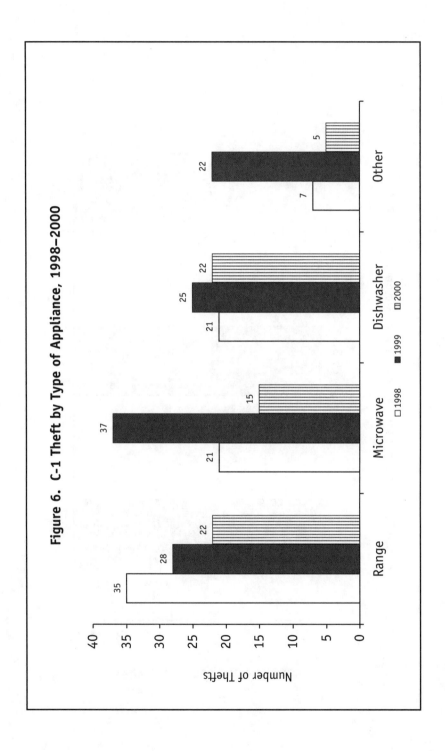

Figure 6. C-1 Theft by Type of Appliance, 1998–2000

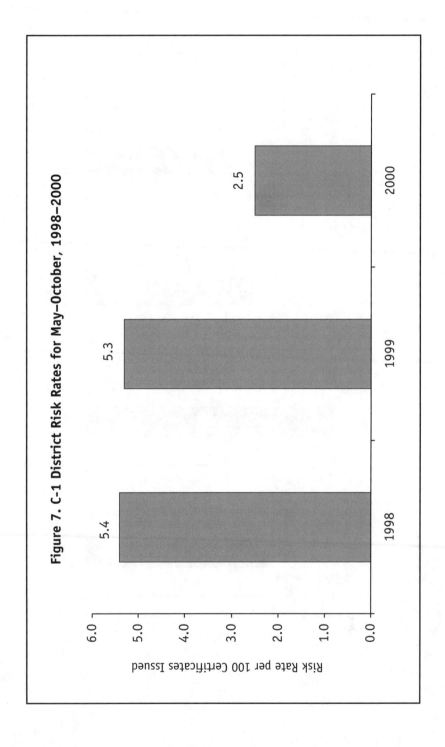

Figure 7. C-1 District Risk Rates for May–October, 1998–2000

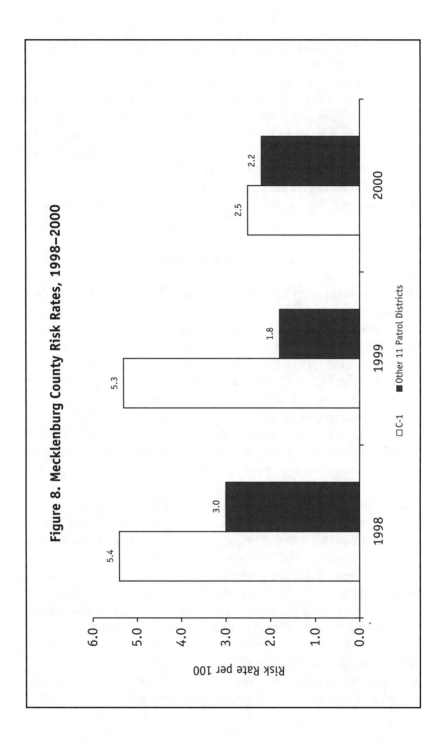

Figure 8. Mecklenburg County Risk Rates, 1998–2000

the year (a rate of 2.4). This project possibly prevented 110 burglaries in the year 2000 alone.

During the first six months of 2001, the officers conducted four more rounds of field checks and continued to maintain records on appliance burglaries. Examination of risk rates indicates the benefits of the project continue. The C-1 appliance burglary risk rate for the first six months of 2001 was 3.5, slightly higher than during the test period. The officers have noticed, however, that the same noncompliant builders keep getting victimized, perhaps because they persist in installing appliances as much as a month before closing.

LESSONS LEARNED

One of the first and most important lessons Officers Cunius and Rost learned from conducting this project was law enforcement alone was ineffective in reducing the problem. Despite the officers' significant efforts in 1999, which resulted in 18 more cases cleared than in 1998, the number and rate of burglaries increased.

The second lesson the officers learned was the large amount of research necessary to analyze the problem. Rost and Cunius had to understand business practices, conduct environmental analyses, determine construction patterns, identify crime prevention methods already in place, ascertain the scope of the problem, locate data resources, clean data and examine enforcement efforts. This knowledge proved beneficial during presentations to builders; the officers were able to speak their language, prepare the presentation in a way that answered many of their questions and counter builder arguments against compliance. By the time the officers made the presentation, they were confident the proposal was workable.

A third lesson was the value of conducting a thorough analysis of crime statistics before implementing a solution. This information lent support to requests for builder participation and made assessment of the solution much easier. The officers knew what data they needed to gather and how to arrange it. They did not have to search for preimplementation data and did not waste time gathering unnecessary assessment data. Comparing the preimplementation data with the assessment data was relatively quick and easy.

A fourth lesson was the amount of determination and persistence required to complete the project. Each step had its roadblocks, ranging from a lack of accurate data to working with uncooperative builders. Team members tackled problems pertaining to their roles and worked to circumvent or overcome the obstacle. The project required a great deal of energy, time and dedication, especially on behalf of Officers Rost and Cunius.

Finally, the officers recognized that police remain the major stakeholder in this problem. Builders are hesitant to make permanent policy changes, possibly because profits are relatively unaffected by appliance theft or due to fears of falling behind competitors. In the year since completing the six-month assessment, several participating builders have become lax in their security; the number and rate of burglaries is again on the rise. Fortunately, those statistics still have not returned to preproject levels.

FOOTNOTE

This project is ongoing. The officers are developing an updated PowerPoint presentation for Chief Stephens to present to the City Manager's executive cabinet and the City Council's Public Safety Committee. Chief Stephens hopes to garner their support in getting all CMPD builders to delay appliance installation to reduce opportunities for theft.

SHOWDOWN AT THE PLAYGROUND:

A Community Confronts Drug and Disorder Problems in a Neighborhood Park

Valerie Spicer and Jean Prince

SCANNING THE SITUATION

Grandview Park is one square block of green space at the center of Grandview-Woodland, a diversified community in Vancouver, British Columbia. The park is on Commercial Drive, the neighborhood's main road, and doubles as a backyard for a variety of people and purposes. The park is also adjacent to a large community center that houses an elementary and high school, day care center and various community services.

Park activities can lift the neighborhood up—or drag it down. The Grandview-Woodland Community Policing Centre (GWCPC)[1] tries to balance law enforcement with an understanding of community standards and tolerances. The GWCPC identified park problems by

- studying citizen complaints and reports,
- examining the area and its social dynamics,
- observing conditions at the park,
- discussing the park with the community, and
- surveying the community.

---

[1] The GWCPC is staffed by volunteer community members who work closely with police to address neighborhood problems. See this chapter's Appendix A for more information.

Reports to the GWCPC regarding park problems were consistent from 1995 to the summer of 1998. These problems, although significant enough to merit action from the center, did not make the park a top police priority.

GWCPC board members, staff and volunteers live in the neighborhood. Their visual observations of the park enabled the GWCPC to evaluate the nature and scope of problems. The neighborhood police officer patrolled the area on bicycle, concentrating on the park. The GWCPC also held several meetings on Grandview Park with residents, business owners, and municipal and community agencies. These meetings helped everyone understand the variety and range of problems, as well as their impact on the park and neighborhood.

In addition, the GWCPC conducted an extensive survey in 1997. About 1,000 people were contacted on the streets, at restaurants, at home, at businesses and in the park and given a written survey. More than 700 responded—an unusually high rate of return. The survey disclosed the community's tolerance for different behaviors in the neighborhood (e.g., drugs, prostitution, noise, parking, bongo drumming and a host of other issues), giving police and civic leaders a clear baseline for their efforts to restore order and civility. The GWCPC also determined that local residents were primarily concerned with problems caused by transient youths camping in the park. Each summer, youths travel to Vancouver (by either backpacking or driving in campers) to pick fruit and plant trees or use the park as a hang out. They play bongo drums, let their dogs run loose, litter, urinate, drink alcohol and smoke pot—all in public.

One year later, however, more serious problems arose. During the summer of 1998, reports to the GWCPC began to include sales of hard drugs. The GWCPC conducted a new survey focusing on what was wrong at the park and what could be done to set things right. Based on the survey responses, the GWCPC concluded the primary problem was the influx of criminal elements from the neighboring Downtown Eastside community—an area plagued by drug use and drug dealing.

By the end of July 1998, the degradation, hard drug dealing and incivilities in Grandview Park had markedly increased residents' fear of crime. Community members visibly retreated from the park, and the number and nature of reports to police and the GWCPC reflected their deepening concern. The GWCPC declared a state of emergency in Grandview Park.

ANALYZING THE PROBLEMS

To respond properly to the array of problems in the park, police analyzed

- social dynamics and problem population movement within Vancouver,
- the park structure and its effect on criminal behavior, and
- police response to park problems.

The Downtown Eastside, about 20 square blocks, is one of Canada's poorest neighborhoods. It also has one of the highest intravenous drug user populations and HIV infection rates in North America. Dealers there visibly sell crack and heroin; users also operate in the open. The area is between downtown Vancouver and working class neighborhoods such as Grandview-Woodland. As the Downtown Eastside is gentrified, with available low-cost housing quickly diminishing, its population is being displaced to other low-rent areas in Vancouver. They bring visible intravenous drug use, overt drug dealing, street prostitution and public incivilities.

Grandview-Woodland, a working-class community with an artistic component, is also undergoing gentrification. The population is highly diversified, and the housing stock provides a range of options—making the locale attractive to Downtown Eastside residents. Public transportation links the two neighborhoods, which also contain similar social agencies. Population movement between these two areas, therefore, is quite natural.

In June 1998, police renewed efforts to control the criminal element in the Downtown Eastside. Some of the dispersed crack dealers and clients moved to Grandview Park. Reports to the GWCPC of crack and heroin sold in the park confirmed this influx of some Downtown Eastside drug traffickers and users. The GWCPC worried that the Downtown Eastside drug dealers and users would tear apart the quality of life in Grandview-Woodland.

Once the crack dealers joined Grandview Park's marijuana dealers, the GWCPC took a closer look at how the physical environment facilitated the drug trade. Particularly helpful in this respect was a 1997 study by Simon Fraser University criminology students of people's interaction with the park environment, which uncovered several design flaws (e.g., bush overgrowth, poor pedestrian path design, poor placement of park benches and run-down park equipment).

Reports to 911 helped the GWCPC and police gauge the success of police responses to problems in the park. All too often, the manner in which calls were cleared by patrol included "gone on arrival," "unable to locate," "unfounded" or "no report." Clearly, reactive police efforts had failed to correct park problems. The park needed a proactive approach.

Drug dealers exacerbated the common park problems of graffiti, litter, excessive noise and unleashed dogs. To address drug dealing properly, the other problems—though pale in comparison—also had to be resolved.

The GWCPC concluded that a concerted effort of several agencies was necessary to control drug activity and took up the responsibility of directing a reversal of the trend. Through the media, the GWCPC in August and September 1998 asked the community to reclaim Grandview Park.

RESPONDING TO THE CRISIS

A broad coalition including local law enforcement, social services, businesses, community members and the media (see this chapter's Appendix B) came together to create "Showdown at the Playground." Project partners sought to

- ensure the community's safe return to the park,
- find long-term solutions for park problems,
- involve the community in the problem-solving process,
- maximize park usage for the widest range of community members,
- establish and maintain community standards through a visible presence,

- redirect delivery of police services, and
- coordinate agencies in delivering services.

Specific responses involved several partners and tactics and were phased in over two years. Strategies included initiating new law enforcement responses, improving the environment, fully involving the community and coordinating agencies and services.

New Law Enforcement Responses

Faced with the significant increase in reports of drug dealing—especially crack cocaine—Constable Jean Prince organized several plainclothes operations to identify dealers. Community members willingly opened their houses to police officers for observation points. Park Watch volunteers (see below) provided police with information on drug deals and dealers.

To stop people from sleeping in campers on a street adjacent to the park, the Neighborhood Integrated Services Team (see this chapter's Appendix B) lobbied successfully for "No Overnight Parking" signs. This was a new ordinance and was enforced by police and city by-law enforcement officers.

On a less successful note, the city Park Board tried to have bongo drummers and area residents agree on a limited, set time for music. The GWCPC even posted signs with timetables. It was soon evident, however, that the primarily transient bongo drummers would not adhere to time constraints.

Improving the Environment

Judging by the graffiti and litter, the GWCPC realized the people who had taken over the park had little concern for it. The GWCPC asked the Park Board for immediate action to control graffiti and litter. Within a week, the Board and Britannia Continuing Education created "Spruce the Drive," hiring youth to pick up litter, remove graffiti and paint murals. Project workers spend one day a week in the park.

Information collected during the plainclothes operations helped horticulturists realize how the park should be changed to eliminate opportunities for dealers to hide drugs. They eliminated obstructed sightlines, severely pruned covered areas and removed low bushes that facilitated hiding drugs.

In October 1998, the Park Board began replacing the sod in Grandview Park. This work involved fencing off green space, which channeled all activity—including drug use and dealing—to the playground area. By December 1998, complaints to the GWCPC and 911 calls indicated major problems in the playground. The GWCPC sought to disperse drug users by trimming bushes, altering the playground equipment and relocating park benches.

Involving the Community

Realizing the park needed to be maintained as a positive community focal point, the GWCPC in 1999 approached project partners to ask for help with a Park Watch project. This summer program has volunteers patrolling the park, observing activities but not confronting drug dealers.

Through the media, the GWCPC invited area residents to reclaim the park by using it regularly. The Britannia Community Centre Children's Committee also arranged family events in the park. The combined effort was named "Put the Grand Back in Grandview Park."

The GWCPC displayed photographs and text at the park to document the progress in reclaiming Grandview. The library, a block from the park, also displayed the text and photographs for a month. This community education effort informed area residents of changes to the park and built their confidence in returning to the park.

Coordinating Services and Agencies

While police were conducting foot and bicycle patrols, Animal Control stepped up its enforcement of unleashed, unlicensed and unmuzzled dogs. The Park Board and the Britannia Community Centre contributed staff and organized park cleanups and mural painting in the park.

Because of the success of Park Watch, the Park Board suggested the GWCPC move its office into the vacant park caretaker's house in Grandview Park. The GWCPC completed the move in May 2000.

ASSESSING THE PROJECT'S SUCCESS

The positive results from "Showdown at the Playground" are multi-faceted. Most important is the heightened sense of community ownership of the park. At each phase of the project, local residents responded to GWCPC requests to help save the park. The GWCPC also received the prompt and willing participation of various community agencies.

Park Use

The most telling measure of success is actual use of the park. Assessment of the population base before and after the response shows a marked change in park users. Before the response, drug dealers and their clients dominated the park. Few children used the playground; local residents walked around the park, not through it. By the end of September 1998, the GWCPC had drastically reduced the number of drug dealers using the park for business transactions. As the drug trade fell off, parents began bringing children back to the playground, and area residents returned to the park for strolling and casual use.

911 Calls for Service

During August and September 1998, the highly visible response caused a marked decrease in 911 calls. During August 1998, police received 37 calls to 911 for service to the park; in September 1998, that number dropped to six. Similarly, calls to the GWCPC concerning the park went from five in August 1998 to zero in September 1998.

Environmental Changes and Police Response

The success of the Crime Prevention Through Environmental Design (CPTED) modifications to the playground also can be measured by use of the area. The goal of modifications was simply to move drug dealers away from the play equipment to another section of the park. Police knew they could not entirely eliminate the drug element, but they were intent on keeping drug paraphernalia and other unseemly discards away from the playground and children.

One modification, for example, involved a playhouse where drug users shot up. When its roof was altered so it wouldn't provide cover for rain, the dealers abandoned the tiny structure to children. As a result of the modifications, drug dealers were successfully moved to an area in the park far from the playground. Park equipment previously used for criminal activities is now used for its expressed purpose; landscaping, once a cover for crime, is now well maintained.

In addition, Park Board statistics show a significant increase in time spent by horticulturists in Grandview Park. Park Board staff horticulturists had previously spent minimal amounts of time and effort in the park, feeling their efforts would be wasted on a dingy environment and that anything they planted would likely be trampled or destroyed. Increased time and cost for park horticulturists is a positive sign, as it indicates more time being spent trimming bushes and tending to park aesthetics (see Table 1).

One goal of the initiative was to increase the effectiveness of police responses in the park. Information collected by the Park Watch helped achieve this end. Examination of 911 calls for service also indicates solid success: Police increased arrests, warrant arrests and drug seizures (see Table 2).

Moreover, proactive police work increased significantly. Table 3 compares calls generated by police on patrol versus calls generated in reaction to public complaint.

The monthly number of dispatched calls during the summer of 1998 was 19, falling to 13 the next summer. An assessment by month found that July accounted for the most significant change. Police reported 15 dispatched calls in July 1998, but only 3 the next year. Comparison of these two summers reveals an inverse relationship between dispatched calls and calls generated by police and Park Watch (see Table 4.).

Although reports to the GWCPC did not decrease from July 1998 to July 1999, these calls contained specific and detailed information useful for subsequent CPTED modifications and police enforcement.

FURTHER ASSESSMENT

Bongo drum complaints declined after the "No Overnight Parking" signs were erected. From May to August 1997, 40 percent of

Table 1. Increases in Cost of Park Staff Time, 1997–99

1997	1998	1999
$14,544	$19,075	$21,750

Table 2. Frequency of Park Arrests and Drug Seizures, Summers 1997–99

	May–Aug. 1997	May–Aug. 1998	May–Aug. 1999
Arrests	0	4	15
Warrant Arrests	1	3	8
Drug Seizures	4	14	30

Table 3. Calls Generated by Police vs. Dispatched Calls, Summers 1997–99

	May-Aug. 1997	May-Aug. 1998	May-Aug. 1999
Police-Generated calls	13	23	52
Dispatched Calls	Not known	19	13

Table 4. Calls Generated by Police vs. Dispatched Calls, July 1998 and July 1999

	July 1998	July 1999
Police-Generated Calls (includes Park Watch)	1	18
Dispatched Calls	15	3

all 911 park calls were for the noise made by bongo drummers; from May to August in 1998 and 1999, bongo drum complaints were only 20 percent of park calls. In addition, complaints to the GWCPC regarding people sleeping and living in the park were nearly eliminated.

Animal Control also noted successful results, stating that Grandview Park is the only park in Vancouver with proactive coordination of services and police. Animal Control statistics show that in 1998, agents issued only one ticket, compared with seven in 1999. Animal Control also seized a drug dealer's pit bull after repeated complaints about the dog and an attack by the dog in the park. The GWCPC continues to observe a marked increase in leashed dogs.

Two weeks after the responses in the park, the GWCPC surveyed 120 community members to assess the impact of park modifications. Findings indicated that a majority of the community had noticed the changes and felt safer in the park.

Although the responses produced the desired results, the GWCPC will continue efforts to improve Grandview Park as a positive community focal point. Another summer of Park Watch, continued visible police presence, community events and the presence of the GWCPC office should build on previous successes. Establishing solid community standards and informing both new residents and service providers will help maintain a sense of order and community ownership.

APPENDIX A: THE GRANDVIEW-WOODLAND COMMUNITY POLICING CENTRE

The Grandview-Woodland Community Policing Centre (GWCPC) opened in April 1995 inside the Britannia Community Centre near Commercial Drive in the City of Vancouver, British Columbia. Volunteers partner with the Vancouver Police Department to manage the GWCPC office, which serves as a resource for both the community and the department.

The GWCPC Board of Directors consists of local residents, business owners and workers. A paid civilian coordinator staffs the office and runs a variety of programs. A constable serves as liaison between the GWCPC, the police department and the community. The constable's primary function is to collaborate with community and government agencies and with the GWCPC Board of Directors and its staff to develop and implement problem-oriented projects that target community issues or concerns.

Impetus for the GWCPC came directly from the community. A group of residents saw a need for this type of police service and approached the police department with an implementation plan. Active collaboration between the community and the police is implicit in every project undertaken by the GWCPC.

Neighborhood problems (drugs, noise, loitering, prostitution) are brought to the attention of police with reports from concerned citizens to the GWCPC. Most complaints involve problems that cannot be solved through traditional, reactive policing. A proactive, problem-oriented policing approach identifies specific concerns. Supporting information is then gathered (through crime analysis or information from various police squads and city departments), and a comprehensive solution is proposed, reviewed, implemented and assessed.

APPENDIX B: PROJECT PARTNERS

Grandview-Woodland Neighbourhood Integrated Services Team

City workers from Police, Fire, Planning, Permits and Licenses, Social Services, Park Board, Library Services and Environmental Health meet once a month to discuss local problems and to develop and implement integrated solutions.

Vancouver Animal Control

Prior to the project, Animal Control worked independently and responded to complaints from the public. Through the park project, the police and Animal Control developed a working partnership.

Vancouver Board of Parks and Recreation

The Park Board provided the GWCPC with staff time to develop a training manual for Park Watch volunteers, hired playground leaders to work with the police and Park Watch volunteers, and participated in community meetings and CPTED modifications to the park.

Britannia Continuing Education

The group instituted "Spruce the Drive," a program to hire youth to pick up litter, remove graffiti and paint murals in the park. Britannia Continuing Education tailors its programs for specific neighborhoods and is under the umbrella of the Britannia Community Centre, which is financed by the city to oversee numerous social programs.

Britannia Out of School Program

Representatives participated in community meetings and suggested solutions to neighborhood problems. The Britannia Out of School Program concentrates on youth and is associated with the Britannia Community Centre.

Eastside Family Place

Family Place, as its name implies, concentrates on strengthening the bonds of family. Representatives participated in community meetings and helped devise solutions to neighborhood problems. Family Place, also associated with the Britannia Community Centre, directs its efforts to preschoolers and single mothers.

Children's Committee

A unit of Britannia Community Centre, the committee lobbied Britannia for a staff person to organize weekly events in the park. Representatives from the Children's Committee also participated in community meetings.

Block Watch Members and Local Businesses

These participated in the project by reporting suspicious activity to 911 and the GWCPC. Residents also provided observation points in their homes for undercover police officers.

Simon Fraser University

Criminology students under the guidance of Professor Patricia Brantingham studied the park and provided CPTED recommendations to the GWCPC and Park Board during the planning phase of the renovations.

Local Media

The local media publicized changes in the park. Small, local newspapers were particularly helpful in spreading the word about efforts to clean up the park through broad, recurrent coverage. From such reporting, neighbors learned in detail about the various programs, efforts and goals of police and community leaders. Once informed, neighbors who might otherwise have remained suspicious and aloof eagerly participated in efforts to change the park and Grandview-Woodland. Radio, television and the large city newspapers also reported on Grandview Park. The news coverage helped convey a major theme of the park programs: The community must concentrate not on disciplining individuals, but on altering highly objectionable behavior patterns.

8

ADDRESSING CITY BEGGING USING PROBLEM-ORIENTED POLICING

Nigel Manning

In early 1999, the Staffordshire, England, Police Department restructured to change its policing style to a more locally based problem-solving approach. To that end, the department in April 1999 created a Local Policing Unit (LPU) to cover the Stoke-on-Trent City Centre area. At about that time, the City Centre area experienced a notable increase in street begging. This chapter describes the LPU's problem-solving approach to that problem, the first significant issue we faced.

SCANNING

Street begging actually emerged as a problem requiring attention in March 1999, approximately one month before the LPU debuted. The department identified street begging as a serious issue based on

- an increase in complaints from citizens and customers to police and business owners;
- numerous complaints from bank employees about lone women afraid to use automated teller machines (ATMs), particularly during the evenings, because of the presence of beggars (who targeted specific machines);
- letters of complaint written by citizens to the local evening paper, causing a high level of media and public interest in the issue;
- concerns expressed to City Centre Management and other key strategic figures by potential investors in the area regarding the negative effect large numbers of beggars had on the City Centre's image; and

- pressure by the City Centre Management Partnership Group to address the problem.

Despite rises in vehicle crime and violence in the area, begging was seen as a priority because it contributed to an impression the area was uncared-for and lacked guardianship. During this period, the department also noted other criminals were attracted to the City Centre and retail crime significantly increased from previous years.

The LPU agreed to help develop a solution but strongly resisted the suggestion this issue should be addressed solely by police or any other single agency. We chose to tackle the problem because of

- the risk to potential new investment (£170 million, or $250 million[1]);
- beggars using more intimidating methods, which increased concern;
- the range of worsening crime and safety problems, which posed a credibility issue for the new unit; and
- the chance to show the unit's commitment to structured problem solving in approaching difficult problems.

Once committed to addressing the problem, we called a planning meeting with the LPU Commander, the City Centre Manager and the Coordinator of a homeless outreach team covering the area. This meeting identified key elements of the problem, likely responses and potential participants for an action group. We then invited these individuals—the LPU Commander, a representative of City Centre businesses, the Radio Stoke Action Line coordinator, the City Centre Manager, a project coordinator from the homeless outreach team, a nurse practitioner who works with homeless people, and the Local Authority community safety coordinator and the partnerships inspector—to a problem-solving workshop on begging.

Workshop participants scanned the problem for relevant factors using the problem triangle. Issues were categorized as pertaining to the victim, offender or location (see Table 1).

---

[1] Investment has since been secured for redeveloping one of our shopping areas.

Table 1. Results from the Problem-Solving Workshop

Victim Issues

Public:
- often misguided into thinking they help the homeless by giving to beggars
- presence of beggars may add to public's fear of crime
- people made uncomfortable by sight of people begging

Retailers:
- beggars detract from image of area
- beggars often focus on target locations, deterring customers from certain stores
- frustrated by lack of resolution to known problem
- often suggest (at least superficially) agencies should bend the rules to solve problem

City Centre:
- begging could indicate lack of care about physical environment
- begging could deter investment
- begging could deter visitors from returning
- City Centre management under increasing pressure to do something

Homeless:
- beggars detract from scale and nature of real homeless problem
- homeless people not fully supported by public
- lost opportunity due to lack of clarity—beggars confuse the issue

Police:
- reluctant to take enforcement action because of emotional nature of issue and likely lack of punishment by courts
- energies are misguided—more effort spent justifying position than resolving problem

Table 1. Results from the Problem-Solving Workshop (continued)

Homeless Outreach Team:
- frustrated by homeless beggars not accessing services
- limited by funding issues
- concerned public is unaware of problem's scale
- concerned some addicts pose as homeless beggars to fund drug dependencies

Offender Issues
- regular beggars established in City Centre
- associates may target area if current beggars move on
- drug dependency an issue for those involved
- main offenders reluctant to access support
- beggars at risk of assault/abuse, particularly at night
- taxing (i.e., senior beggars taking a cut from other beggars for "allowing" them to work in a particular area)
- beggars also are crime victims

Location Issues
- high volume of pedestrian public
- high levels of cash (e.g., near ATMs, bus stations)
- recognized "pitches" (i.e., same beggars using same location on daily basis)
- relatively pleasant/interesting environment for beggars
- both day and evening activity
- City Centre very close to potential areas of support
- risk of increased opportunity for begging in nearby Cultural Quarter (comprising theatre, bars, restaurants)

ANALYSIS

Workshop results helped us generate several hypotheses. Initially, we analyzed Police Command and Control data to identify begging hot spots. Underreporting and an unwieldy computer system, however, limited that data's value. LPU constables and the Local Authority closed-circuit television station then conducted a street survey to identify locations and times of day that beggars operated in the City Centre. They mapped the survey findings and presented results to the action group, which confirmed and validated the report (see Figure 1, next page). As part of this exercise, constables also identified beggars and shared that information with the homeless outreach team. This work provided accurate hot-spot information linking locations and offenders and offered a basis for future efforts; the survey has been repeated semimonthly to chart project success.

We next conducted face-to-face interviews with local business owners, which confirmed we had accurately identified their views during scanning. Perhaps more important, the interviews bought us time and goodwill, involving our biggest critics at an early stage of shaping our response. We also interviewed members of the public who were seen giving money to beggars and monitored discussions on local BBC radio stations as well as the letters on the subject in the local newspaper. This partly confirmed our workshop findings and highlighted the public's goodwill and willingness to help people in trouble. It also showed their confusion and frustration over the issue, as many wanted to help but did not know the best thing to do. For example, more than half the people spoken to did not make any link between giving money to beggars and the beggars using that money to buy drugs.

The homeless outreach team directed interviews and survey work to examine the true nature of City Centre beggars and homeless people in our area. This work generated the following findings:

- All identified beggars at that time were drug addicts. The survey also identified 10 regular beggars (those sighted most frequently within a certain period of time).
- More than 60 percent of beggars were failed shoplifters who were well known by many City Centre stores and banned from most larger ones.

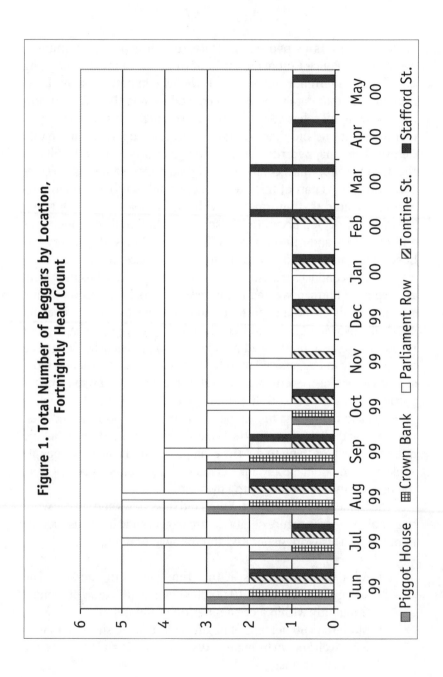

Figure 1. Total Number of Beggars by Location, Fortnightly Head Count

- Begging provided beggars their main source of finance to purchase drugs. It was not uncommon for them to earn £50 ($70) during a good day.
- Homelessness was an issue for around 30 percent of City Centre beggars.
- Habitual beggars had identified pitches (particular begging locations) they protected.
- Taxing did occur between beggars. Occasionally they were violent toward each other and the street drinkers with whom they sometimes associated.
- Low self-esteem was identified as a significant issue. Many beggars did not access support offered by the rough-sleepers team because they had sustainable income for drugs through begging.
- Just under 80 percent of homeless people in the area (and City Centre beggars) originated from the region.

Finally, we brought in a trained crime-reduction officer to perform architectural site surveys (i.e., environmental assessments). These examined pitches to recognize common factors and help us develop location-based responses with more certainty. The surveys confirmed our understanding of location-based issues and highlighted aspects of the locations that could make them attractive for other legitimate activities (e.g., visually enticing environment, customer-friendly, high pedestrian traffic).

We had hoped to measure begging's impact on business and profits but were unable due to the sensitive nature of this information. Even so, our analysis indicated begging was a growing problem. Without some intervention, the situation would only worsen—not just in relation to begging, but in other areas due to the "broken windows" aspects associated with this problem.

Following the analysis, the LPU set the following objectives:

- Significantly reduce the number of on-street beggars operating within the City Centre area from figures recorded during the first three months following the launch of our project. (We did not specify a target number because we felt City Centre should ultimately have no beggars but knew this was not achievable.)

- Divert habitual beggars toward more healthy lifestyles via support at a local drop-in center.
- Raise public awareness of homelessness and begging.
- Raise funds to support homeless charities and projects and reduce public funding of beggars' drug habits.

RESPONSE

Given the complex nature of the problem, we decided a broad-based, holistic strategy would be most effective. We did not wish merely to displace the problem or change the behavior to other unlawful activities. While the main priority was reducing the problem, we also wanted to provide an exit strategy for people involved in begging.

We favored this kind of holistic response strategy because we felt

- it would deliver the best long-term value,
- a single-agency response was inappropriate and would be very limited in its success,
- it was a more socially and morally acceptable course of action than enforcement campaigns that would split public support either for or against beggars and mask some of the real issues, and
- specific targeted and tailored support was essential due to the diverse range of problems and needs of the offending group.

We sought to gain ownership of the response both within and outside the force by involving people on the front line in shaping the project, showing the situation could be improved, creating opportunities for positive press and media coverage, displaying strong leadership and commitment at a senior local level, and celebrating and promoting success while being honest and objective enough to admit when we got things wrong. The ownership and involvement of the people at the center of the project—the beggars themselves—was seen as critical for long-term resolution.

To start, we examined good practices nationwide to see how other towns and cities had addressed this growing problem. Unfortunately—

and surprisingly—we did not find an "off-the-peg" solution or strategy we could readily implement. Through the Association of Town Centre Management, we did find one practice that could possibly fulfill two elements of our strategy: Winchester's "Make-It-Count" program, which sought to divert public donations from street beggars toward charity. We decided to follow Winchester's lead by conducting a public awareness campaign and providing collection boxes throughout City Centre. This program did not, however, target support and enforcement for habitual beggars or address the location issues identified in our analysis.

As part of our response to target support and enforcement for habitual beggars, we used original research to create a file for each identified beggar. We also established an information exchange protocol between the LPU and the Potteries Housing Association, which manages the homeless outreach team and drop-in center outreach workers. Unfortunately, our goal of introducing shared multiagency negotiated care plans went unrealized when we lost the coordinator due to funding cuts. These plans remain on hold at the time of writing but will be resumed if we have a significant return of beggars.

We provided information to businesses experiencing the most problems with beggars and developed a "professional witness" statement for recording instances of antisocial behavior before contacting police. We also targeted beggars who had consistently refused support from the outreach team, while referring them to the drop-in center in an attempt to both reduce their income and push them toward seeking help.

In other responses, we highlighted begging pitches for the Local Authority Markets Inspector (responsible for street trading in the City Centre) and began classifying them as either busking[2]/street entertainment pitches or street trading pitches. We also identified all ATM areas as zero-tolerance zones for begging, policing this policy firmly and consistently. We communicated this to all beggars via the outreach team and personal contacts.

---

[2] Busking is the practice of entertaining (particularly by singing, dancing or playing an instrument) in a public place, often along a busy street.

It took a fairly long time to locate appropriate collection boxes. Meanwhile, the City Centre Manager organized and developed a week-long coordinated marketing and information campaign for official launch in November 1999. Besides radio, TV and newspaper coverage, the campaign included large posters placed around the City Centre in advertising panels and on litter bins; these highlighted the presence of collection boxes and told the public "Begging Is Not the Answer."

The diversion of public donations to the charity boxes soon reduced income from begging significantly. Some beggars began to access support, seeking prescriptions for their addictions and visiting the drop-in center more regularly. The next stage of this process—development of a fast-track drug rehabilitation arrangement—is in progress.

As we got to know some of the beggars, we even developed individual strategies. For example, one young female beggar received a clarinet and musical tuition. Once she reached an acceptable standard, she auditioned and was given a permit to work in the City Centre as a street entertainer, busking rather than begging for income.

Of course, no POP effort is without challenges. We encountered several difficulties during the development and introduction of our strategy. After about three months of really good progress, for example, we stagnated for a couple of months waiting for updates from other stakeholders. We eventually took the initiative by making our own arrangements. When we introduced street entertainment into one of the best begging locations before fully informing beggars, a young female mime artist was "taxed" for working the pitch. This occurred only once, but it highlighted the importance of integrating strategies. Finally, as mentioned above, the program lost a key person—Gary Thomas, the rough-sleepers project coordinator—for lack of funding. This unexpectedly halted development of negotiated care plans.

ASSESSMENT

We decided independent evaluation by an external body was too expensive and would offer limited value. Instead, the action group compared both soft and hard data to gauge the project's success.

As part of our ongoing monitoring of the project's impact on the number of street beggars, we

- continued the semimonthly street survey by the City Centre Manager,
- monitored progress and amended the plans or strategies as needed at periodic steering committee meetings,
- identified a formal review date, and
- organized a survey of businesses and the public. (To obtain a more accurate view, we chose not to conduct the survey close to one of the planned publicity weeks, when the large display posters promoted the project.)

Our assessment highlighted several successes. First, the number of incidents per month involving on-street beggars dropped from roughly 18 to about 5 over the half-year since the project's introduction in November 1999 (see Figure 2, next page).

Since initiating our response, use of the drop-in center by the target homeless group has increased 30 percent; we must note, however, the drop-in center introduced numerous improvements during this period, so the increase in usage cannot be directly linked to the project. The LPU also raised public awareness of the issues involved in begging, the link between begging and drug misuse and the basis of the project. On a less successful note, 60 percent of the core habitual beggars simply moved on and are now begging in other towns.

We administered two surveys to City Centre businesses and visitors that identified several trends:

- City Centre customers were far more aware of the project and its success than managers and workers of shops and businesses,
- 92 percent of the public surveyed had heard of the project,
- 64 percent of businesses had heard of the scheme,
- 94 percent of the public had noted some or vast improvement, and
- 48 percent of businesses had noted some or vast improvement.

Among business owners surveyed, those located in areas of previously heavy on-street begging were significantly more aware of the

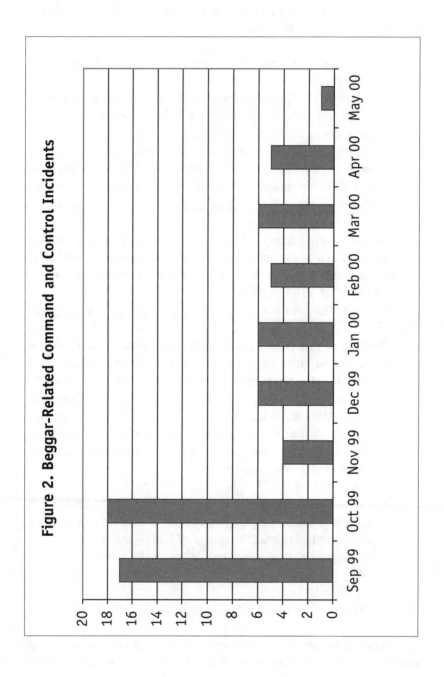

Figure 2. Beggar-Related Command and Control Incidents

project, saw in the main a vast improvement and felt the project to be successful. Business owners not directly affected by the begging problem were less certain of the project's success and felt the situation was mostly the same—or even, for a few, worse.

The collection boxes we installed raised finances for homeless charities and drug referral work. We project an annual income of £3,000 to £5,000 ($4,000 to $7,000) from the boxes, though this depends on how effectively we promote their use during peak periods (e.g., winter, Christmas). This is lower than Winchester's intake (about £14,000 or $20,000 per year), perhaps due to the high volume of tourists visiting that city. We will carry out additional work during the year to establish this with more certainty so we can amend our strategy accordingly.

Finally, favorable locations for begging are now used for other purposes. Principal City Centre sites are now essentially self-policed, with no drift of begging back into them. We will continue the semimonthly head counts and conduct further survey work with the public.

This project has been promoted nationally by Home Secretary Jack Straw as being good practice. It also has won the first-ever Staffordshire Police Problem-Solving Award and is promoted countywide as good practice in terms of both tactics and approach.

We have identified additional work to test our hypothesis that beggars have displaced because they want to continue their current lifestyle in a different location, rather than access available support and change how they live. This additional work will involve tracking identified street beggars to see where and how they have moved on so we can identify why this occurred and refine our strategy accordingly.

Future developments and project spin-offs will include support for longer-term work on preventative strategies based on current research by the drop-in center team. We accept we will probably always be catching up to our end of this problem and are unlikely ever to resolve completely the social situations that cause people to beg. We remain upbeat about our project, though, and will continue to modify, improve and learn from it as circumstances change in the field.

9

IMPLEMENTATION OF PROBLEM-ORIENTED POLICING IN LANCASHIRE

Stuart Kirby

INTRODUCTION

Lancashire covers 1,185 square miles and has a population of nearly 1.5 million (see Figure 1, next page). The Lancashire Constabulary is divided into six command units (A–F), employing 3,300 officers and 1,500 civilians.

In 1997, the new Chief Constable of Lancashire was charged with setting the constabulary's direction and aims. The challenge she faced was deciding what policing style could deliver her aspirations. During this period, the Chief Constable invited Professor Tilley of the Police Research Group to describe problem-oriented policing (POP) to an open forum at Lancashire Police Headquarters. At the end of that presentation, the Chief Constable concluded the constabulary would examine POP in greater detail. Based on our experiences, this chapter provides a template for POP implementation that may benefit other agencies.

THE DECISION TO USE POP

Initially, research focused on whether POP was a viable operational style to introduce. A task force used formal project management methodology to scrutinize such police forces as Leicestershire, Cleveland, Thames Valley, Surrey and Strathclyde—all of which had committed considerable resources to this philosophy. The task force also consulted with the Police Research Group and other academics. A wider review, using the Internet and resources of the Police Execu-

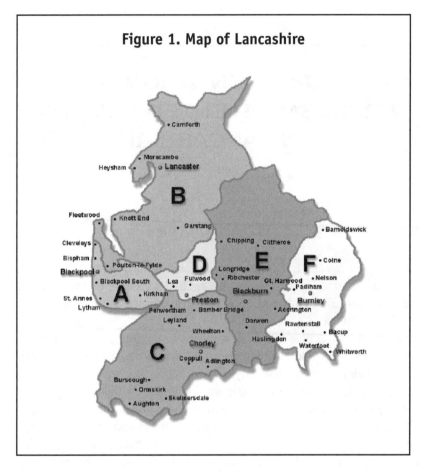

Figure 1. Map of Lancashire

tive Research Forum (PERF), led to a 12-day visit with the San Diego, Calif., Police Department for technical assistance.

A subsequent meeting of Chief Officers and Divisional Commanders decided the business case for implementing POP had been sufficiently made, based on six principal reasons:

- POP is consistent with the style of policing the Lancashire public wanted; it is community-focused and involves a partnership approach.
- POP was inevitable. Forthcoming legislation (the Crime and Disorder Act) would statutorily require police and local government to cooperate on community safety initiatives.

- POP provides a viable strategy for reducing public demand for police services.
- POP provides a framework for more effective policing.
- POP allows more cost-efficient policing.
- Finally, POP works. Police forces implementing this approach effectively have reduced crime/disorder and overall demand for police services.

This group also made the significant decision to implement POP holistically. This meant bringing POP to all officers rather than using a tiered approach that segregated problem-solving officers. Concerned that so many police agencies had tried and failed to implement this approach, the task force next outlined required changes and assessed the impact such changes would have on the constabulary.

IMPLEMENTATION ISSUES

All organizations the task force reviewed confronted consistent strategic issues. After analyzing their efforts, the task force concluded successful implementation depends on quality staff who know their part within the organization, who have the tools to deliver, who are allowed to deliver, who want to deliver and who *do* deliver outputs and outcomes. The following sections indicate how each of these strategic areas involve considerable levels of change.

Quality Staff

Research in the United States and England suggests those attracted to police work are more suited to traditional enforcement than a community approach, which uses partnerships to solve problems. This means examining such issues as recruitment, induction, selection, reward and appraisal prior to implementation.

Who Know Their Part in the Organization

Those employed to deliver problem solving within the constabulary must have clarity of role and purpose. The Chief Constable, therefore, had to define the purpose of the approach explicitly for her staff, as well as the competencies she expected from constables, sergeants, inspectors and superintendents.

Who Have The Tools to Deliver

Analysis at this stage identified many problem-solving tools. Most important, staff needed to be empowered and be close to their community, as such resources are most effective when locally controlled. Second, Information Technology systems must supply accurate and timely information. For the constabulary, this meant merging crime and disorder records. Further, there was the critical issue of partnerships and the ability to implement them successfully at strategic and tactical levels. Finally—overarching all of these—analysis revealed the organization needed to harness and spread good practices (i.e., manage knowledge) for POP to be most effective.

Who Are Allowed to Deliver

Identifying and producing the tools is effective only if staff are allowed to use them. Therefore, leadership was identified as one of the most crucial aspects to successful implementation. The constabulary also had to manage and prioritize public demands so officers could proactively identify and solve community problems.

Who Want to Deliver

This area includes organizational culture. The author's own longitudinal study of new recruits replicates other results found nationally. Specifically, it shows police officers moved from a service-minded approach to a perspective that was internally focused and biased toward enforcement. Clearly, plans to reverse this cultural indoctrination are required.

Who *Do* Deliver Outputs And Outcomes

How do police forces know their inputs (i.e., their officers, vehicles and policing strategies) are linked to their outputs and eventual out-

comes? Effective methods of audit and evaluation are crucial. Another important issue the analysis highlighted was that service provided should be ethical.

With this list of implementation issues, the task force examined
the force's current status (i.e., carried out a "present position audit")
and conducted a risk assessment of potential barriers and their impact on implementation. Some of the risks were significant. The switch
to geographical policing, for instance, frequently diluted resources
and created officer safety issues; many forces had moved away from
this type of structure. The task force then created a contingency plan
for each highlighted risk. One instance would be the informal weekly
meetings between staff associations and the Deputy Chief Constable
to dispel rumors quickly (e.g., changes in service or staff). The review
also provided a checklist of success factors so everyone in the constabulary would recognize successful POP implementation.

IMPLEMENTING POP

Once analysis was complete, implementation followed the same level
of planning. Representative teams from each division and department
(including commanders, constables and support staff) attended a two-
day workshop. Using the strategic framework mentioned earlier (quality staff, who know their part in the organization, etc.), the teams
developed one- and three-year plans projecting the changes they
would make to embed POP within their part of the organization. These
plans led to unprecedented changes in systems and processes throughout the constabulary, which moved forward in a coordinated fashion.

Quality Staff

The constabulary's human resource department reviewed and changed
the recruitment process to sustain the community problem-solving
philosophy. External consultants, constables, sergeants, inspectors
and superintendents developed a competency framework setting out
required POP-related behaviors. Additionally, the POP philosophy was
infused into all induction and selection processes. Recruitment for
specialist posts, including detective posts and promotion to sergeant,

now involves questioning all staff about their involvement and understanding of problem solving. Headquarters and some divisions offer open learning centers (rooms where officers can access problem-solving training packages via the Internet, CD-ROMs and videos). Probationary constables are required to complete a problem-solving initiative during training, for which a reward system was initiated. For example, the winner of one annual competition got to attend PERF's International Problem-Oriented Policing Conference. Similarly, chief officer commendations have changed to acknowledge work that is partnership- as well as law enforcement-based.

Who Know Their Part in the Organization

The force developed quantitative and qualitative objectives to focus the constabulary on problem solving. Quantitative objectives for POP officers include reducing crime, disorder and nuisance, and road casualties. Qualitative elements have evolved over the past three years and relate to public satisfaction and confidence. The force also re-evaluated roles to ensure they added value to community problem solving and filled priority front-line posts to support POP. The constabulary produced a video for staff that presented examples of POP initiatives, showed community members the benefits of POP, and featured the Chief Constable professing her commitment to POP. Each division and department provided training so all staff understood their part in this philosophy. A monthly internal newsletter continually dedicates space to highlight the POP approach. Finally, the force gave POP presentations to all stakeholder groups and the community.

Who Have the Tools to Deliver

To promote ownership and local identity, the constabulary restructured the force by geographic area, each under the direction of a geographic inspector. Divisions shifted as much of their resources as possible to the control of these geographic areas; budgets were devolved to division and departmental control. Staff in geographic areas received training in such topics as financial management. To facilitate local problem solving, the force identified and studied discrete communities. Consultation groups regularly offer their views on problems in the community and various policing issues.

Each geographic area and support department set individual plans and targets. Two analysts in each division provide relevant and timely information on recurring incidents and trends. Areas also share reported crime and disorder information daily. An intranet database for sharing good practice contains (at the time of writing) 180 initiatives. The force also has held three problem-solving conferences with guest speakers (e.g., winners of the Herman Goldstein Award for Excellence in Problem-Oriented Policing) from the United States.

Who Are Allowed to Deliver

After examining call-handling centers and deployment issues, the force decided to decrease its communication rooms from 14 to 6 centers. During this process, it is pushing to prioritize calls and deploy officers to the most critical incidents. Moreover, the force is developing processes to resolve demand for service at the earliest opportunity, as well as considering volunteers to assist with community problems.

A SARA (Scanning, Analysis, Research, Assessment) form helps officers problem solve, and new directories identify suitable partners at the strategic and tactical level. Local officers are acknowledged for getting involved in partnerships at a tactical level. Joint training has taken place with partners, albeit not on a systematic basis. The Lancashire Partnership Against Crime is a registered charity providing funds for community problem-solving initiatives (e.g., youth shelters). Since April 1999 it has provided £91,000 ($133,000) to projects with a problem-solving approach to reducing crime and disorder.

Who Want to Deliver

Interventions are transforming the force's organizational culture to one that facilitates problem solving; leaders are selected based on their understanding of and commitment to the philosophy. Chief Officers regularly state their commitment to POP to staff and stakeholders—even if their officers breach a local protocol (e.g., provide restricted information to the media).

Who *Do* Deliver Outputs And Outcomes

The force has articulated the importance of ethics and values in its strategy and established an ethics working group. Checks and balances are in place to audit such issues as crime reporting. A rigorous performance management structure holds people accountable for community problem solving; this structure starts with the Association of Chief Police Officers and follows a tiered approach to divisions, departments, geographic areas and individuals through the Performance Development Review process (the annual appraisal process for all staff).

ASSESSMENT

Thorough and honest evaluation has been critical to the implementation process. The force made many lower-level assessments during 1998 and 1999. For instance, POP conference organizers assessed the 200 participating operational officers and established that the different training methods had increased their awareness of POP. Similarly, the POP training project—also formally managed—had an evaluation written into the process.

It was felt, however, that formal evaluation must be independently conducted at three levels. The most important criterion was outcome. POP implementation is not an end in itself; it must make a difference to the communities of Lancashire. In the two full years since implementation, Lancashire has seen a reduction in crime, disorder and crime-related fatalities. Similarly, customer satisfaction is reported at high levels. Crime rates display a measurable difference in performance. Between 1992 to 1993 and 1997 to 1998, the Lancashire Constabulary recorded a 10.7 percent reduction in crime—considerably below the national average reduction of 17.9 percent. During 1998 to 1999, however, the constabulary showed the largest reduction of crime in the country (10.1 percent against the national average of 1.4 percent). This trend continues and is revisited later in the chapter.

Still, POP's contribution to the decrease is unclear. The second level of evaluation, therefore, examined whether the force had achieved the critical POP success factors outlined in its original project (e.g., increased levels of awareness, senior officer commitment, local structures, rewards). A team from the District Audit department met with chief officers, circulated 350 questionnaires (receiving a 50 percent response rate) and conducted focus groups with operational officers from all divisions and headquarters. Results provide an overview of progress across all divisions and headquarters, highlighting areas where significant progress had or had not been made. It showed that though the constabulary had come a long way in embedding POP within the workforce, more progress remained to be made. One significant finding was that the division most accepting of POP experienced the most success at crime reduction (9.3 percent in the first year and 12.5 percent in the second year).

The assessment so far had shown the Lancashire Constabulary's performance was improving and POP systems had been implemented. But what of the quality of the POP initiatives? Were they making a difference within the community? Anecdotally, the force heard many success stories about longstanding problems finally being tackled. Similarly, the constabulary entered more examples (16) than any other force for the first Tilley award (the British equivalent to the United States' Herman Goldstein Award), earning commendation as a runner-up. Lancashire presented three papers at the second British POP conference and sent three operational officers to PERF's 1998 International POP Conference. The force also assisted the national development of POP through numerous presentations to other forces and its presence on the National POP Working Group.

In a 1998 national review of Community Safety partnerships, Her Majesty's Inspectorate of Constabulary (HMIC) described only 5 percent as ultimately successful. Given that finding, Lancashire decided a more detailed evaluation would benefit the constabulary and reviewed all problem-solving initiatives within one division for a full year. Each of the division's 46 initiatives were analyzed as to whether they

- involved a particular partner,
- were community-focused,
- were based on crime prevention theory,
- had clear objectives,
- had evaluation criteria,
- had sufficient resources,
- had been evaluated,

- had been successful,
- provided sustainable solutions and
- had an exit strategy.

External bodies such as the Audit Commission, Crime Concern and HMIC emphasized the importance of these variables.

The subsequent, statistically validated analysis highlighted a number of important issues. In a significant improvement on HMIC findings, 33 percent of the initiatives were successful. Of course, this meant 67 percent did not result in sustainable reductions of crime/disorder—a terrible waste of resources. Many potential partners, such as the County Council, Health Authorities, victim groups, help groups, minority groups and the environment agency, were poorly utilized; only partners closest in proximity to the problem were likely to be used (i.e., local authority, schools, local business).

The majority of initiatives (71%) had clear objectives and were community-focused, due in part to the SARA model's structured problem-solving approach. Sustainability correlated positively with initiatives that were innovative, had proper resources, were theory-based, had clear objectives and evaluation criteria, and involved more than one partner. This corroborated the findings of HMIC, Crime Concern and (most recently) the 1999 Audit Commission. The force therefore created a simple checklist to help officers implement initiatives. Finally, sustainability correlated negatively with partnerships intensive in police resources.

GOING AROUND THE LOOP AGAIN: USING SARA TO IMPROVE POP IMPLEMENTATION

The three levels of assessment showed the constabulary had done a significant amount of work in implementing POP; the force recognized, however, that the implementation process was dynamic and should start again. The desired outcome remained the same: All staff would implement problem-oriented policing to help achieve the force's objectives—notably to reduce crime, disorder and road casualties and improve public satisfaction and confidence.

The scanning process had remained constant. Lancashire representatives were members of a national working group liasing with other forces, and the second national POP conference had provided information still not fully analyzed. The District Audit department report also was extremely useful, showing the level of commitment to POP across the force, within individual divisions and at headquarters. This coincided with the arrival of a new Deputy Chief Constable from another police force who was committed to POP and had fresh ideas. As a result, a forcewide steering group, comprising divisional representatives and operational headquarters departments and chaired by the Deputy Chief Constable, met to discuss the way forward.

Analysis

The steering group's main issues related to increased visibility and commitment from senior managers, enhanced intelligence systems to support the process and the effective spread of good practice. Representatives agreed to analyze their part of the organization, consult with staff on their division and produce an action plan.

Response

Based on the steering group's analysis, the force implemented the following responses:

- All items for management meetings (including those for chief officers, divisional commanders, operations managers, etc.) are now submitted using the SARA format.
- At each monthly operations managers meeting, a divisional representative shares a problem-solving example from the division with colleagues.
- All divisions and the two main operational wings of headquarters have submitted action plans on developing POP in their area. The plans identify POP coordinators at the force, division and geographic area levels.
- The constabulary has compiled a corporate policy setting out responsibilities for implementing POP.

- Divisional commanders nominate officers implementing effective community problem-solving initiatives for a commendation from the Chief Constable.
- The central database for sharing POP good practices has been
audited and edited to improve quality.
- The force developed a briefing system that downloads vital
information (e.g., intelligence, warrants, custody system,
crime and incidents) from a number of databases so officers
can obtain detailed briefings on a particular geographical area
at the touch of a button. (This system was recently highlighted
as good practice by HMIC.)
- The steering group continues to meet regularly to explore
new methods of achieving its established objectives.

Assessment

These more recent responses have invigorated Lancashire's approach
to POP. For the first time, officers routinely receive Chief Constable
commendations for partnership initiatives. The force has a more coordinated approach to problem solving based on recognition of the
different levels at which it can be accomplished (e.g., individual, geographic area, divisional, force).

Again between 1999 and 2000, crime and disorder rates dropped
in Lancashire while rising in many other areas across the country.

CONCLUSION

This chapter has tried to show the considerable effort needed to trans-
form good practice (in terms of problem solving) into common practice across an organization comprising approximately 5,000 people.
No doubt we have insufficiently outlined the considerable difficulties
in traveling this path, the debates over geographic policing, empow-
erment and culture being particularly significant.

The Policing and Reduction of Crime Unit (formerly the Police Research Group) and other police agencies in England have argued the
Lancashire Constabulary's implementation of POP is unique because

- it explicitly articulated the benefits prior to implementation;
- it affected all individuals within the force, as well as a significant number of other agencies;
- implementation was systematic, following a formal project management methodology;
- evaluation involved independent assessment of all divisions and departments by the District Audit office; and
- the process can be linked to enhanced performance.

One final critical point is that the constabulary has continued to move forward in POP, reiterating the SARA process on a forcewide basis a number of times. It now coordinates regional, force, divisional and geographic area POP responses. This method of thinking— coupled with passage of the Crime and Disorder Act—continues to open up new possibilities. We hope this chapter provides other forces a template that can serve as a starting point when they consider implementing the POP philosophy.

REGIONAL PROBLEM SOLVING USING THE NATIONAL INCIDENT-BASED REPORTING SYSTEM

Donald Faggiani, Dan Bibel and Diana Brensilber[1]

Law enforcement's ability to monitor hot spots of crime and anticipate changes in patterns of offending provides important opportunities for proactive prevention strategies that use scarce resources most
effectively. Crime mapping and other analysis techniques for identifying crime patterns over time and location also support problem-
oriented policing efforts (see La Vigne and Wartell 1999). At the local
agency level, these tactical crime-mapping efforts are enhanced significantly by a well-designed incident-based reporting (IBR) system.
Such systems permit monitoring of incident location and time, weapon
use, types of structures and other characteristics that can identify
shifts in offending and reveal emerging patterns or trends within the
locality.

The same advantages from mapping crime within one jurisdiction apply to mapping across multiple jurisdictions. Over the past
decade, research has shown that offenders have become more mobile, making identification and arrest more difficult. As offending
patterns have changed, it has become increasingly important for law
enforcement to move beyond boundaries and collaborate in multijurisdictional efforts. Multiagency regional crime mapping can identify patterns of offending that would otherwise go undetected, such
as displacement activity or regional crime series.

This type of interagency tactical planning can also be used to
address emerging crime problems. As we have seen from the crack

[1] The authors would like to thank Judy Lim, from the Police Executive Research Forum, for preparing the maps and helping with other analyses used
in this chapter.

cocaine epidemic, certain patterns of offending are more prone to rapid expansion. While a locality may be able to monitor growth within its own boundaries, understanding the regional implications can help thwart a rapid expansion across jurisdictions. Thus, routine monitoring of local and regional trends can help identify changes in offending patterns and serve as a multijurisdictional early warning system.

Unfortunately, as Eck (2000) notes, multijurisdictional crime mapping has encountered numerous obstacles. Often, information simply is not shared among law enforcement jurisdictions. Any sharing accomplished is generally through an informal process on a case-by-case basis or through aggregate-level summary statistics, limiting the information's utility for regional crime mapping. There are only a few examples of several agencies within a region joining to form a regional crime mapping system (see La Vigne and Wartell 2001). While these rare efforts typically are successful, they require significant resources and time to achieve their goals.

This chapter

- examines how the FBI's standardized IBR systems can help surmount several multijurisdictional data-sharing obstacles;
- demonstrates how the Commonwealth of Massachusetts, by enhancing its statewide incident-based reporting system, overcame many barriers to regional crime mapping; and
- discusses several data quality issues critical to obtaining reliable results when sharing data among jurisdictions.

CROSS-JURISDICTIONAL CRIME ANALYSIS

Effective regional crime analysis efforts should optimally build on partnering agencies' existing incident-based Records Management Systems (RMS). Given today's rapid technological advances, it might seem the answer is simply to merge all agencies' systems into a centralized data set for mapping cross-jurisdictional incident-based data. As Eck (2000) notes, however, the reality of data sharing among jurisdictions is not always a simple task; differences in technology and data compatibility limit the development of regional crime mapping and analysis systems. In general, a local law enforcement agency's RMS is designed to serve the needs of the locality, not to support regional law enforcement efforts. As a result, the technical design of one agency's RMS may make that system incompatible with those of neighboring jurisdictions. The FBI's National Incident-Based Reporting System (NIBRS) is being tested as a viable solution to the data-sharing problems historically encountered with local attempts at regional crime mapping and analysis.

THE FBI'S NATIONAL INCIDENT-BASED REPORTING SYSTEM

The FBI developed NIBRS to replace the Uniform Crime Report (UCR) summary crime reporting system, which collects only a snapshot of information on the overall serious crime situation within local police agencies. Data collectors (police) and data users (everyone else) have long lamented the difficulty of collecting UCR data and its limited usefulness for crime solving and informing public policy. Except with homicide, for example, no information is collected on crime victims. It is, therefore, impossible to identify the characteristics of such high-profile issues as juvenile or elderly victimization, domestic violence, or the influence of drug or alcohol involvement.

NIBRS removes many of the older UCR system's limitations by collecting data in which the criminal incident, rather than a group of incidents, is the basic data source. This provides a wide variety of information on victims, offenders and arrestees, offenses, and property—allowing for true policy-relevant analysis. While NIBRS is designed as a national crime statistics database, it also can serve as the basic foundation for a local law enforcement RMS. The intent is to provide standardized, incident-level information consistent across all law enforcement jurisdictions—yet ensure that the information is still useful at the local agency level. The resulting data set is an invaluable asset to local law enforcement, other governmental organizations and criminology researchers. From a problem-solving perspective, NIBRS has several investigative uses—including tactical and strategic crime analysis, as well as rudimentary criminal investigative analysis.

One of the most interesting strengths of address-specific crime data is its ability to help police and policymakers examine crime distribution and patterns across political boundaries. Faggiani and McLaughlin (1999), for example, used 1997 NIBRS data from Virginia to examine trends in the sale/distribution and possession of narcotics. They found NIBRS provides "significantly more incident-related detail than has heretofore been available for strategic crime analysis at the regional or state level. Moreover, NIBRS provides neighboring communities the opportunity to compare information on crime patterns that may extend beyond local boundaries." While their study used data from four noncontiguous jurisdictions and serves only as a conceptual example, it is significant in that it lays the groundwork for further research in this area.

As demonstrated in the following sections, federal implementation of NIBRS will enable a variety of topical analyses—far beyond what is possible with previous crime data collections. But an even richer analytical system can be achieved by adding a small number of data elements at the local level. This enhanced system is more in tune with local needs and mandates, while also expanding our understanding of the dynamics of crime and offending.

DEVELOPMENT OF THE
MASSACHUSETTS IBR SYSTEM

The Massachusetts State Police Crime Reporting Unit developed the foundation for statewide and multijurisdictional crime mapping and analysis by using NIBRS data submitted by local police agencies. Though the FBI provides specific instructions on the structure and format of NIBRS data submitted by state crime-reporting programs, each state is free to add additional data values and variables to meet local needs or practices. Many state programs have added offense data using the state's own coding scheme. Others add data values to existing data variables for more specificity (adding, for example, new values for victim-offender relationship or extra categories of hate-bias motivation).

In Massachusetts, one such enhancement to NIBRS was the addition of incident address. Though NIBRS does collect information on 'location type,' this field describes only the type of location (e.g., residence, street, convenience store, etc.). Without a specific street address, the lowest level of geographic disaggregation possible is the agency jurisdiction.

Collecting incident address enables accurate crime mapping. While large agencies can use crime mapping as an operational or tactical tool, even small to medium-size agencies (which are the majority of agencies submitting NIBRS data) can find it useful. These communities may feel they do not need crime maps because everyone knows where crimes are occurring, but all police agencies can benefit from examining a wide range of crime area characteristics. Accurately mapped crime data can be merged with other data sources, such as census and public works information (location of street lights, bus stops, etc.). Research has shown that changes to the physical environment can reduce crime. Identifying and addressing negative physical patterns in high-crime areas can help eradicate crime and disorder.

Massachusetts worked closely and cooperatively with the Massachusetts Chiefs of Police Association on implementing the federal NIBRS data set to ensure their input and support for this major revision in crime reporting. Full information about the NIBRS data set was provided to the Association, along with the rationale for moving away from the old summary crime reporting system. The Association's Executive Board was assured the state would continue to operate a voluntary submissions system and continue to accept summary data (provided that was the only way a department could submit it). As a result of this informative process, the Executive Board voted to accept NIBRS as the new standard for crime reporting in Massachusetts.

The NIBRS structure presented to the chiefs in Massachusetts generally follows the federal standards, though the Massachusetts program did explore incorporating several modifications. These were in response to both state statute (concerning the scope and detail of bias crime motivations) and feedback received from meetings of police officials and other concerned parties.

EXPLORING THE USES OF MASSACHUSETTS NIBRS DATA

The NIBRS data set, as specified by the FBI, contains a rich variety of data elements, and it was clear the data could be useful at the state level for a number of policy-relevant analyses that would have been impossible using summary crime data. Address information can add significant value, but the data must be geocoded—given a specific latitude and longitude (or x and y coordinates) based on the street address. The software used to do this will impute (or estimate) the coordinates based on information in its database. Once the data are geocoded, the state can make the data available to smaller police agencies that often do not have the staffing, technical expertise or equipment (hardware or software) for mapping.

In 1998, the Massachusetts State Police Crime Reporting Unit began exploring incident mapping using NIBRS data. Although neither address data nor coordinate information were collected on the state level, local data contributors had incident address data. As an experiment, the city of Worcester provided the State Police Crime Reporting Unit with NIBRS-submitted incident case numbers and corresponding addresses for 1995.[2] This data file was then merged with the incident data and geocoded for mapping. The success of this test process confirmed the viability of mapping NIBRS data; what remained to be seen was how many departments could analyze the data.

In the late 1990s, the Massachusetts Statistical Analysis Center began conducting an annual survey on the status of police technology in the state. Along with questions about local police departments'

---

[2] Worcester was selected as the test site for a number of reasons. As the second largest city in Massachusetts, it reported a reasonably large number of NIBRS incidents to the state program—typically about 2,000 each month. Worcester had been a NIBRS contributor since 1995, so its data quality was consistently high (in terms of the errors uncovered by the state's NIBRS repository). The FBI also certified its data was of high quality based on a 1998 Quality Assurance Review; this process indicated the sample of cases reviewed had an error rate of less than 2 percent. Finally, the department at that time had some internal capacity for crime analysis but not for mapping.

hardware and software, the survey inquires into departments' capacity for crime analysis and mapping. Survey results are roughly comparable to those of the Crime Mapping Research Center's 1997–1998 national survey (see Mamalian and La Vigne 1999): Most large departments have both crime analysis and mapping programs, but the number of agencies with either program decreases as department size decreases.

The majority of police departments supplying NIBRS data to the state are these smaller agencies with neither crime analysis nor mapping capacity. This reinforced the Crime Reporting Unit's interest in using NIBRS to develop an enhanced system of crime analysis and mapping. By incorporating address information, the data set could be the basis for a comprehensive analytical tool for police agencies. When informed that the collection of address information would facilitate regional crime analysis, state chiefs of police without question or hesitation voted to support the modifications to include specific address details. Police software vendors were informed of the change, which was implemented by March 1999.

USING NIBRS TO IDENTIFY
LOCAL CRIME PROBLEMS

Having committed to the modifications, the authors faced an important question: Could the enhanced NIBRS data be used to overcome the issues restricting data sharing for regional crime mapping and analysis?

To address this research question, we examined a target area of Worcester and eight adjacent jurisdictions. This area was selected for two reasons. First, all communities reported IBR data to the state police for the entire time period of the study (July 1, 1999 through June 30, 2000). Second, while Worcester is the second largest city in Massachusetts, the adjacent jurisdictions are all relatively small and unlikely to maintain separate crime mapping and analysis units within their departments.

Analyzing a Regional Problem

The Criminal Information Section of the Massachusetts State Police identified a drug trafficking route of concern between Woonsocket, Rhode Island, and Worcester. In addition, anecdotal information suggested Worcester was a nexus for drug sales, specifically heroin, in the region. Using this information, we begin our analysis by examining all drug-related incidents in the target area. Table 1 shows that, in Worcester, heroin-related incidents[3] are more prevalent than even marijuana incidents (36 percent of drug-related incidents in Worcester involved heroin; 28 percent involved marijuana).

In 1999, 38 law enforcement agencies in the United States serving populations greater than 100,000 reported data through NIBRS. As Table 2 (see page 164) shows, the rate for heroin-related incidents in the target area was disproportionately higher than for all other agencies. In fact, Worcester had the second highest incident rate for heroin of the 38 agencies (the only agency with a higher rate was Springfield, Masschusetts). The next highest city had a heroin incident rate of only 31.6 per 100,000 population. Agencies adjacent to Worcester also had a disproportionately higher rate of heroin-related incidents than all other agencies reporting NIBRS data in 1999 for populations of fewer than 50,000. Based on the findings from Table 2, the remainder of our analysis focused on heroin-related incidents and arrests in our target area.

La Vigne and Wartell (1999) note that a Geographic Information System (GIS) combining police data with location information in a digital map can be a useful problem-solving tool—it helps identify specific types of crimes and distinctive elements present in multiple incidents. In addition, they note a GIS can assist in "breaking incidents down to identify a specific problem, trend, or pattern" (312). Figure 1 (see page 165) maps heroin-related incidents for the period July 1999 through June 2000 for Worcester and the adjacent jurisdictions. The map shows a heavy concentration of heroin-related incidents in Worcester, with several heroin-related incidents in Auburn (southwest of Worcester) and Shrewsbury (directly east of Worces-

---

[3] Our initial analysis is at an incident unit of count (i.e., all drug-related incidents reported to police even if an arrest is not made).

Table 1. Drug-Related Incidents in Target Area

Drug Type	Adjacent Jurisdictions	Worcester	Total for Target Area
Crack cocaine	3.6%	10.4%	7.2%
Cocaine	3.9%	19.2%	12.1%
Heroin	8.0%	35.9%	22.9%
Marijuana and other cannabinoids (e.g., hashish)	72.3%	28.2%	48.8%
Other narcotics	3.2%	0.7%	1.8%
Other drugs	2.1%	1.1%	1.6%
Unknown drug type	6.9%	4.4%	5.6%
Total	**100%**	**100%**	**100%**

Numbers may not add exactly to 100 percent because of rounding.

Table 2. Mean Heroin, Cocaine and Crack Cocaine Incident Rates by Agency Size*

Agency Size	Heroin	Crack Cocaine	Powder Cocaine
All agencies reporting NIBRS data to FBI in 1999			
Fewer than 50,000	2.73	36.88	18.05
50,000 to 100,000	3.68	54.39	18.70
More than 100,000	15.74	92.42	28.47
Total	**3.02**	**38.75**	**18.27**
All reporting jurisdictions *without* target area (Worcester and adjacent jurisdictions) in Massachusetts			
Fewer than 50,000	2.63	36.97	18.08
50,000 to 100,000	3.68	54.39	18.70
More than 100,000	12.39	93.23	26.90
Total	**2.86**	**38.82**	**18.27**
Target area (Worcester and adjacent jurisdictions)			
Fewer than 50,000	29.79	13.64	9.49
More than 100,000	139.90	62.24	86.55
Total	**43.56**	**19.71**	**19.12**

* Rates per 100,000 population.

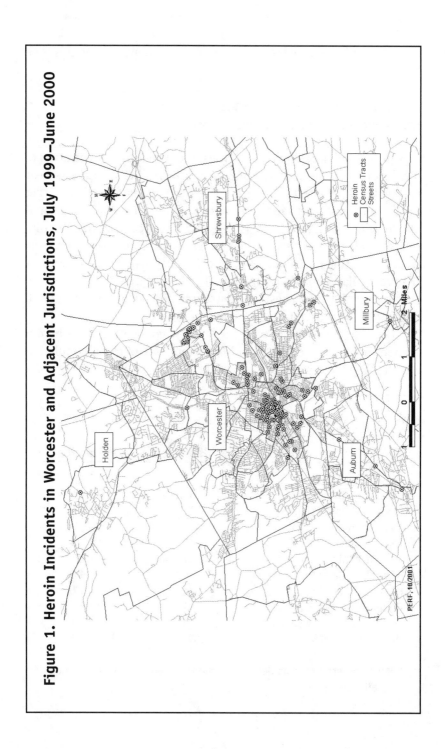

Figure 1. Heroin Incidents in Worcester and Adjacent Jurisdictions, July 1999–June 2000

ter). Many adjacent towns also have single incidents during this time frame.

Heroin-Related Incidents in Worcester and Shrewsbury

As Figure 2 (next page) demonstrates, the heaviest concentration of incidents involving both sale and possession of heroin appears near the center of Worcester. This region encompasses five of the target area's 41 census tracts and accounts for 57 percent of heroin-related incidents in Worcester. There is also a heavy concentration of heroin-related incidents on the northeast side of the city, with one census tract accounting for 15 percent of incidents. In Worcester, 45 percent of heroin-related incidents are for sale and distribution. The six census tracts with the heaviest concentration of incidents account for 70 percent of sale/distribution incidents in the city.

The six census tracts with the highest concentration of heroin related incidents account for 13.6 percent of the city's population (see Table 3). Relative to the rest of the city, these six tracts are char-

Table 3. Demographics for Worcester

	Hot Tracts	Rest of City
Percent Population	13.6%	86.4%
Percent Property Crime	30.0%	70.0%
Percent Violent Crime	36.4%	63.6%
Population per Sq. Mile	11,814	7,079
Percent Black*	11.9%	3.1%
Percent White*	61.5%	91.8%
Percent Hispanic*	34.6%	5.1%
Percent Other*	26.7%	5.1%
Percent Owner-Occupied	4.3%	17.6%
Percent Vacant Households	6.1%	2.8%
Median Housing Value	$109,683	$121,865

* Race and ethnicity, as defined by the U.S. Census Bureau, are not mutually exclusive.

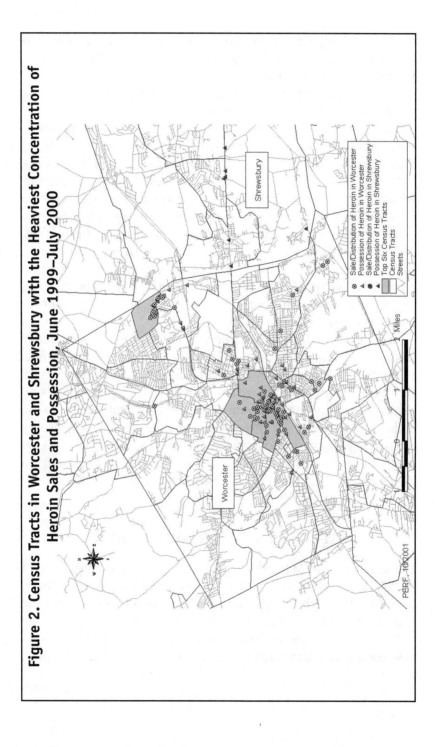

Figure 2. Census Tracts in Worcester and Shrewsbury with the Heaviest Concentration of Heroin Sales and Possession, June 1999–July 2000

acterized by a higher population density, lower percentage of owner-occupied housing units and higher percentage of vacant housing units. The median housing value is also lower than for the rest of the city. These same areas account for 30 percent of all property crime and 36 percent of all the violent crime in the city.

In their analysis of street-level drug markets, Weisburd and Green (1994) found sale and distribution of heroin more likely along major thoroughfares and intersections. According to the NIBRS data, 61 percent of all heroin-related incidents in the target area occurred on highways, roadways or alleyways. Figure 3 provides an exploded view of central Worcester showing sale (circles) and possession (triangles) of heroin. Similar to the findings of Weisburd and Green, the majority of these incidents occurred along a major thoroughfare in Worcester—in fact focused on a 15-block stretch of Main Street in the center of town. As we will discuss shortly, this type of information can be important for problem-solving efforts.

While Shrewsbury (population 27,000) does not have many heroin-related incidents, its rate is relatively high. Two patterns in Shrewsbury become apparent from Figure 2 (previous page). First, all heroin incidents in Shrewsbury are related to possession—no heroin-related sale or distribution incidents. Second, similar to the findings in Worcester, the majority of heroin incidents in Shrewsbury occur along major roadways.

All persons arrested in Shrewsbury were nonresidents, while in Worcester 87 percent of those arrested resided in the city.

CRITICAL DATA-QUALITY ISSUES

The experience in Massachusetts demonstrates the potential of a regional approach to crime analysis and mapping. Here and elsewhere, collecting data with comparable data elements and values, reporting that information to a centralized database and providing it to all contributing agencies can be a powerful crime-fighting tool. To make best use of these data, however, several data quality conditions must be met.

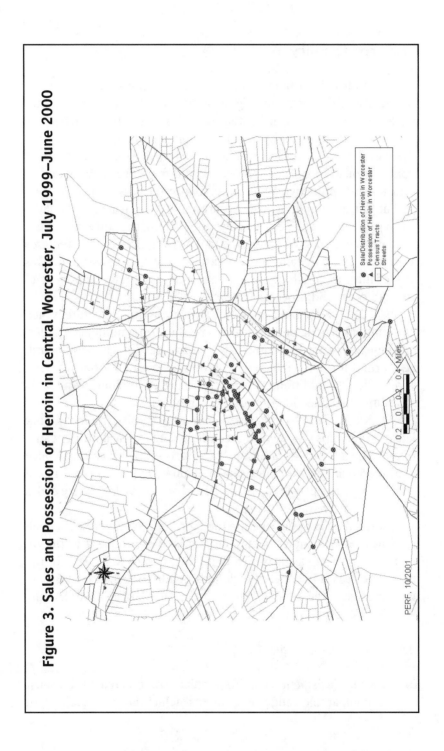

Figure 3. Sales and Possession of Heroin in Central Worcester, July 1999–June 2000

Sale/Distribution of Heroin in Worcester
Possession of Heroin in Worcester
Census Tracts
Streets

0.2 0 0.2 0.4 Miles

PERF, 10/2001

Uniform Quality

While all police departments collect data with some degree of detail, the quality of data can vary significantly based on different agency needs. For example, agencies that use data to inform proactive police work (such as planning and decision-making) require more complex data than agencies focusing on more reactive responses (such as rapid response to calls for service). Rapid response requires only a fast car, while proactive policing needs good historic data.

Further, even though many departments have an automated RMS, which requires data be entered into the system, the software cannot mandate the quality of entered data. Ensuring data quality requires consistent and constant internal case review and assessment. This type of internal feedback and review is an essential component of any data entry and processing system.

Also, agencies should share data with a common structure. When collecting, analyzing and interpreting data from a number of different agencies, conflicting formats jeopardize data quality. A standardized format for data collection will increase data uniformity among all agencies. In addition, all agencies must have similar standards governing the collection of routine crime data.

The Massachusetts IBR system has various edits and mandatory data relationships that govern acceptable data for each incident submitted. The system requires age, race, sex, ethnicity and residence status variables be submitted for individual victims, and each field must have an acceptable value. (Each field does have legitimate codes for missing or unknown values.)

There are, however, no edits that consider aggregate data-quality issues. For example, it may be legitimate to code a victim-offender relationship as unknown. But when this code is used for the majority of cases in which the victim's gender is female and the offense is aggravated assault, the quality of the data as a whole must be called into question.

Uniform Coverage

The data each jurisdiction uses to populate combined data sets must cover a comparable range of incidents, which is often difficult to achieve. The police relationship with citizens varies in different communities based on a variety of factors and does affect the type of data collected. For example, a department that has worked to improve lines of communications with the community may have a high proportion of reported offenses; in another agency with a poor citizen relationship, only more serious offenses may be reported.

Police-community relationships are only one facet of this problem. A community with a large number of non–English-speaking residents may have less crime reported due to language barriers. Moreover, some recent immigrants may come from countries where police are viewed as agents of repression rather than sources of assistance.

Jurisdictional Tolerance for Problems

Other jurisdiction characteristics influence the type of data maintained by the police department. For example, in a community with a high crime rate, the agency may file written reports only for the most serious incidents. By prioritizing responses, these agencies are better able to deal appropriately with the immediate, critical incidents facing their community. By contrast, a community with a lower rate of offending may expect the police to respond vigorously to all incidents, no matter how minor. The fact that all offenses, no matter how minor, are not officially recorded in some agencies may make regional crime analysis more difficult.

Uniform Data Policies and Practices

Technical issues notwithstanding, internal agency policy and policing practices also can limit information sharing. The following internal agency policies can have important consequences:

- **Data-sharing protocols**. Agency protocols may prohibit or limit the sharing of some information critical to finding patterns or offenders. For example, concerns over privacy and disclosure of names and other personal identifiers pose conflicts when sharing data across jurisdictions. Localities will need to negotiate these and other concerns (see La Vigne and Wartell 2001).

- **Uniformity of offense definitions**. Regional databases are often compromised by inconsistent agency definitions of offenses (such as aggravated assault).
- **Data appreciation**. One department may better appreciate the value of its data system than neighboring jurisdictions. This agency may expend more resources to maintaining the data system and have more sophisticated systems of data entry and data cleaning.

Policing practices that can affect data include whether the agency is focused on proactive or reactive policing. An agency with zero tolerance for a certain offense, such as marijuana possession, will often have very high arrest rates for this offense. A neighboring jurisdiction, on the other hand, may focus most of its resources on sale and possession of crack cocaine. Comparing arrests for marijuana possession between these two jurisdictions might well show a significantly higher arrest rate for the first agency; this would not necessarily mean, though, that the marijuana problem is more severe in that area.

SUMMARY AND CONCLUSIONS

The standardized structure of NIBRS data transcends the needs of a single law enforcement agency. Neighboring agencies can compare like information on emerging crime patterns and problems that extend beyond local law enforcement boundaries. Access to data from neighboring agencies allows cross-jurisdictional problem solving and crime analysis without requiring complicated interagency agreements for collaboration. Data from neighboring communities can then be used to follow and even anticipate trends.

REFERENCES

Eck, J. E. 2000. Crossing the Borders of Crime: Factors Influencing the Utility and Practicality of Inter-jurisdictional Crime Mapping. Presentation at the Crime Mapping Research Center Conference Series, Washington, D.C.

Faggiani, D., and C. L. McLaughlin. 1999. Using the National Incident-Based Reporting System for Strategic Crime Analysis. *Journal of Quantitative Criminology* 15(2):181–91.

La Vigne, N., and J. Wartell. 1999. Crime Mapping for Problem Solving. In *Problem Oriented Policing: Crime-Specific Problems, Critical Issues and Making POP Work,* vol. 2, edited by C. Solé Brito and T. Allan. Washington, D.C.: Police Executive Research Forum.

La Vigne, N., and J. Wartell. 2001. *Mapping Across Boundaries: Regional Crime Analysis.* Washington, D.C.: Police Executive Research Forum.

Mamalian, C. A., and N. La Vigne. 1999. *The Use of Computerized Crime Mapping by Law Enforcement: Survey Results*. Washington, D.C.: National Institute of Justice.

Weisburd, D., and L. Green. 1994. Defining the Street-Level Drug Market: The Jersey City DMAP System. In *Drugs and the Crime: Evaluating Public Policy Initiatives,* edited by D.L. Mackenzie and C.D. Uchida. Newbury Park, Calif.: Sage.

A NEW GENERATION OF FIELD TRAINING:
The Reno PTO Model

Jerry Hoover, Gerard Cleveland and Greg Saville

BACKGROUND

Imagine giving a young person a car, one that has a powerful engine and is fun to drive. Then take nearly four months and *teach* him this car represents state-of-the art technology and is the only thing on the street worth driving. Now imagine that when he has completed the training in the operation of this fantastic car, we give him a different car to drive. Despite being instructed to the contrary, the car he was trained to drive is too old. It was built three decades ago and doesn't meet society's needs. It is an inefficient gas-guzzler. Today we have a better car: It is more efficient, less costly and better for the community. Of course, it is more difficult to drive and, in some cases, not as much fun. Because we care about our young friend and want him to accept the new car, we offer him the choice of which one to drive. Given that scenario, how many new, efficient cars will be on the street? Very few.

That is exactly what we are doing in law enforcement. But it is not the police car we need to be concerned about; the problem instead is our inability to train new officers who can work under any police philosophy. We presently train most police officers using a model developed in 1968. This model has been the mainstay for police training ever since. Once officers have completed training using a model that does not teach the skills needed to practice community policing, they often are given additional training and asked to "make the choice." The choice they make tends to be the method of policing taught three decades ago. Why? Because it is easier and, to some, more fun.

HISTORY OF A TRAINING PROCESS

Community-Oriented Policing and Problem Solving (COPPS) is quickly becoming the philosophy and daily practice of progressive police agencies around the world. A common concern voiced by police executives in its implementation involves training, especially for new officers. Many practitioners believe training has not kept pace with the rapid changes in the field. The Reno Police Training Officer (PTO) program is a new model for postacademy training that incorporates contemporary adult educational methods and a version of Problem-Based Learning (PBL) adapted for police. This approach to training provides a foundation for lifelong learning that prepares new officers for the complexities in policing today and in the future.

Problem solving lies at the heart of contemporary policing. The problem-solving process strikes at the roots of crime, rather than hacking at its branches. It provides police a more comprehensive understanding of problems through in-depth analysis and guides them in developing tailored strategies with the community. Instead of a simple response to calls on an incident-by-incident basis, problem solving provides a broader model for police operations.

Police administrators have recognized the ineffectiveness of incident-driven policing, as well as the economic insensibility of random patrols, rapid response and postcrime investigation. Racing from call to call—in spite of its appeal on television programs—does not promote good policing. For example, responding to the same domestic dispute nightly or regularly citing the same disorderly youths gathering in a park are ill-considered strategies that communities can no longer afford.

The Reno PTO program is not based on developing mechanical training or rote skills. Static skills, though necessary to police work and an integral part of any training program, do not constitute the primary teaching approach necessary for police agencies implementing more contemporary COPPS practices. We hope organizations will find this model a valuable tool for helping trainees learn to do their job in a fair and competent manner.

The Reno Police Department and the Police Executive Research Forum (PERF) conducted research in the development of this program to identify the key topic areas required in today's policing environment. Police administrators, training supervisors and officers from across the country participated in all stages of program development. This included meetings with experts from various disciplines, a nationwide survey of more than 400 police agencies and a review of dozens of police training manuals. Researchers also examined field training programs from law enforcement agencies across the United States and Canada. Interestingly, 7 out of 10 departments surveyed indicated they used a derivative of the traditional model for field training. This increased to more than 80 percent when considering only departments serving populations of 300,000 or more.

The Reno model uses the phrase *police training officer.* The writing team, including current police trainers and supervisors, deliberately moved away from the language of earlier training models that use the military phrase *field training officer* (FTO). This change of language reflects the movement toward COPPS and an emphasis on PBL in the training process.

Police administrators voice two major concerns with current FTO programs. The first is that, despite local modifications, there has been very little change over the years. Standards for the old FTO model, for example, were written in the early 1970s and modified in 1981 to clarify issues with interrogation and investigation. Not until 1996 were the first community policing standards included as an "add-on" to the basic program. They remain an add-on and alternative to other policing activities.

The second issue with current FTO programs revolves around their ostensible focus on legal issues—in particular liability and termination. At the inception of the traditional model, agency heads thought they needed a training program that would defend them in court against claims of inadequate or insufficient training.

While liability is a major concern of police administrators, experience has shown very few departments have had to use the model for that purpose. Regardless, liability concerns should not drive a training program, though they can be addressed during training. The type of training model an agency chooses does not necessarily reduce liability; methods of applying that training and the guidelines to which officers adhere make the difference.

Agencies using the traditional model also complain that too much time is spent documenting the training due to liability and termination concerns. This is time taken away from training and mentoring new officers. In all fairness to the current FTO program, that is not what is taught. Still, the emphasis on numerical ratings is attractive to agencies concerned about liability, and over-documentation has quickly become a common practice.

There is no argument that agencies need proper documentation for remediation and termination. The problem lies in the dual role FTOs play in this situation. Once a training officer decides a trainee is having serious problems, training typically ceases; the FTO then spends a majority of time building a case for termination. The balancing act between evaluator and trainer is made more difficult by the administrative demands of most current FTO programs.

A NEW MODEL

The Reno program is based on the PBL teaching model and emphasizes the need for the PTO to function primarily as a trainer. PBL is a contemporary training model used in the military, education, community development and medical arenas. It began in the late 1970s and early 1980s, when Dr. H.S. Barrows of Ontario's McMaster University found medical students were entering examining rooms with vast amounts of knowledge but were unable to ask the right questions of patients. Their learning had taken place in classrooms and within the covers of medical texts; when faced with actual patients, the interns often were unable to apply their knowledge successfully to cure patients' ailments.

The point is that medical students do not train simply to learn about diseases or anatomy or pharmacology. They train to help people get better or stay healthy. This is prevention—a concept typically ignored in the past by the medical and policing fields. While medical students need an essential body of knowledge, they also need to know how and when to apply that information effectively in treating patients. Further, students require a system of learning and retaining information they can continue to use throughout their careers as doctors. PBL proved so successful at meeting these demands that numerous medical schools have now adopted its use.

The similarities to policing are striking. Trainees need to learn much more than just the laws and procedures. They must understand how to use their knowledge judiciously and effectively when dealing with people. They must also have a learning guideline they can use each time they encounter different community problems.

Because we ask more from our police today, it follows we must provide them with the resources and training to fulfill their expanded role. The title *law enforcer* is too narrow a mandate or description for any officer working in the United States today. Herman Goldstein pioneered the concept of problem-oriented policing, writing that police objectives in our society span a wide range of activities: protecting against threats to life and property, assisting crime victims, and creating and maintaining communal security. It makes good sense to have police trainees think about roles and responsibilities as they approach specific problems in their daily work. Problem solving is an integral part of most police work and requires creative and flexible thinking. This model facilitates those qualities.

Rationale for a PBL Training Model

There are three main reasons why it became necessary to develop an updated model for postacademy training. First, the current standard for evaluating trainees draws on approaches developed more than 30 years ago; problem-oriented policing and community-based policing were not yet part of the police repertoire. Policing has changed a great deal over the past 25 years, and training systems must change to keep pace.

As discussed, most current postacademy training systems came about because of the need to minimize the agency's liability regarding police behavior. Unfortunately, time has shown these methods neither automatically reduce an agency's liability nor guarantee a smooth termination process. Also, today's postacademy training models often try to compensate for poor hiring/selection processes. This causes the training process to become a documentation-laden effort that sometimes overshadows actual training of new officers. While liability will always be an issue, it should not drive the training function.

It is also important that a training model be flexible and adaptable to local conditions. Most of today's FTO models are boilerplate productions that do not differentiate among agencies. Research for this new model discovered some agencies implementing FTO programs even failed to remove the name of the originating agency in materials. The Reno model is flexible and ensures that agencies personalize the program to their individual needs and capabilities.

Changing Course

Agencies embracing COPPS want trainees to be effective problem solvers—not just knowledgeable about skills, tasks and safety, but able to apply that knowledge to solving crime and disorder problems. Daily checklists emphasizing "passing and failing" scores simply do not help adults learn. Education research has improved greatly over the last few decades, and we now know a great deal more about how adults learn in the most effective way. Police trainers should take advantage of these improvements. Reno's PBL model incorporates long-overdue strategies for training new officers.

Few programs in use today meet the needs of COPPS training. Several attempts to incorporate COPPS training into present models have failed. That is why we chose to build a new model rather than modify an old program.

THE RENO PTO MODEL AND COPPS

Community policing has two components: partnership and problem solving. Partnership is defined by the willingness of police, the public, government agencies, businesses and social service agencies to collaborate in cooperative relationships and share the responsibility for public safety. Partners must have honest relationships if their collaboration is to thrive.

The second component, problem solving, relies on the beliefs that crime and disorder can be analyzed as problems resulting from underlying conditions and that, if these conditions are changed, the problems may be solved. This is a break from the traditional concept of policing. Police in the United States have inherently seen themselves as crime fighters, not problem solvers. Police officers perform a different role as problem solvers: They spend more time eliminating factors contributing to community problems and less time focusing on incident response.

The Need for a Problem-Solving Foundation

Most FTO programs teach skills, knowledge and abilities in separate categories, such as "arrest powers" or "family disputes." Individually, each of these items is indeed an important part of the job. But PTOs complain this kind of training has a formulaic, rigid and report-driven character. It is too easy for trainees to be tested on their performance at individual tasks, rather than on how they deal holistically with a variety of police tasks, skills and knowledge.

In the past, FTOs instructed trainees in specific tasks, checking each off in the critical task manual (or training guide) when completed. Yet events seldom occur as independent actions. Rather, they are complicated affairs in which officers must use discretion in interpreting events, make intelligent decisions and actually resolve problems. This is especially true in problem solving. A checklist does little to help trainees learn to do this.

Training officers often complain that, under current systems, trainees soon discover they can be more successful by doing nothing than by taking action or initiative and risking a failing grade on the daily evaluation. While trainees get daily grades for such incidents as stopping speeding cars, there is no corresponding check mark to indicate whether *ongoing* traffic problems in the area were resolved. Similarly, the trainee may receive a passing score for dealing with pedestrian *contacts,* but less evaluative emphasis is placed on whether this contact had any significant impact on neighborhood crime. The current evaluation system does little to establish a climate for the kind of learning that improves problem solving.

In short, current training and evaluation procedures teach officers to mirror the practices of incident-driven policing. Problem-solving activities have remained adjunct practices, often listed as independent sections on trainee evaluations that simply get checked off when a particular task is completed. Problem-solving study units are tacked onto current training programs as if citizens' needs are somehow not central to policing. The situation is analogous to teaching architects the various sorts of material used in buildings without allowing them time or training to consider the needs of those who will actually live in the buildings.

Problem solving requires a creative and flexible method of thinking that cannot be turned on and off like a switch. It is an integral part of most police work, but checklists do not encourage officers to think of it as such. The Reno model uses a PBL approach to encourage that flexibility and creativity.

Objectives of the Program

The Reno PTO program aims to

- provide learning opportunities for new officers that meet or exceed the needs of both the community and the policing agency;
- develop and enhance trainees' academy learning through a series of "real-life" problem-solving activities within the community environment;
- foster growing independence from the PTO over the course of training, eventually reaching a stage where the trainee can work effectively while alone on patrol;
- produce training program graduates who can provide customer-centered, responsible, community-focused police services;
- teach transferable learning skills using a PBL model that trainees can apply to problems throughout their careers; and
- provide consistent, fair evaluations that measure not only trainees' skills, knowledge acquisition and application, but also their ability to problem-solve effectively.

Refocused Evaluation

The Reno PTO model strongly emphasizes evaluation but departs from existing programs that focus on numerically driven daily evaluation forms. Evaluations in the Reno Model take place informally every day, formally each week and during two phases by an independent evaluator. The trainee also is evaluated on a beat profile and on response to problem-solving exercises. The benefit lies in the fact that evaluations become part of the learning process. Both trainee and trainer are responsible for evaluating trainee behavior because the evaluation process becomes part of the new officer's learning activities. After implementing the new model, agencies find forms less time-consuming for trainers and more powerful and effective as training tools.

This change in evaluation focus also offers an increased ability to terminate unsuccessful trainees. The self-evaluation components provide an honest reflection of the trainee's difficulties in the program that are difficult to dispute.

So How Does It Work?

This training program is designed to enable trainees to excel in all forms of police work. If agencies define police work as catching bad guys, handing out speeding tickets and breaking up bar fights, this training system will teach officers to do those things. If agencies define police work as dealing with gangs, helping victims and going to court, this training system will still work. No matter how you define police work, this PBL model will help trainees learn to do that work in the most effective way.

Under the Reno model, trainers assign "street" problems to trainees and have them learn about policing in the context of solving those problems. Trainees work through responses with their PTO's help. Developers of the Reno model surveyed more than 400 law enforcement agencies to identify current priority activities for officers in COPPS-oriented departments. Based on the survey results, the Reno model is structured around Four Modes of Policing, each of which has certain Core Competencies. The Four Modes of Policing are Patrol Activities, Nonemergency Response, Emergency Response and Criminal Investigations.

Within each mode, officer activities are identified as consistent Core Competencies. Trainees are expected to meet department standards for competency in each of the following areas: Police Vehicle Operations; Use of Force; Report Writing; Problem-Solving Skills; Local Procedures, Policies, Laws and Philosophies; Officer Safety; Ethics; Cultural Diversity; Conflict Resolution; Leadership; Individual Rights; Community-Specific Skills; Communication Skills; and Self-Awareness and Self-Regulation.

The Reno PTO program offers a 16-week schedule:

Week 1   Integration week (acclimating the trainee to the police environment)

Weeks 2–4	Phase A: Patrol activities
Weeks 5–7	Phase B: Nonemergency response
Week 8	Midterm evaluation period
Weeks 9–11	Phase C: Emergency response
Weeks 12–14	Phase D: Criminal investigation
Weeks 15–16	Final evaluation

Each phase of training focuses on a mode of policing. During each phase, the trainer/trainee team responds to calls for service. As trainees respond to calls, they learn the skills and tasks covered under that phase's core competencies.

Implementation

The Reno Police Department implemented its PTO model in May 2001; four other national sites are preparing for implementation in the last quarter of 2001. Reno PTOs report their trainees are learning at a quicker pace and willing to take on learning problems and issues earlier than experienced under the traditional FTO model. (See Table 1 for a more detailed comparison of the traditional FTO and the Reno PTO programs.)

SUMMARY

Traditional models of police training based primarily upon evaluation and litigation concerns have served law enforcement well enough over the last three decades, but they no longer meet the needs of contemporary policing. PBL models have been successfully used in many fields of study to enhance learning and performance and are well suited for police postacademy training. The Reno model will help agencies better prepare their new officers for the challenges of today's policing environment.

For more information on the Reno PTO program, contact PERF at 202-466-7820.

Table 1. Comparison of Traditional FTO and Reno PTO Training Models

Structure of Program	Traditional FTO Model	PTO Model
Commitment from Chief Executive	Unqualified.	Same.
Location of Program Control	Patrol division.	Same.
Responsibility for Program (Rank)	Lieutenant reports to Division Chief. Others are excluded.	Mid-manager reports to Patrol Division head. Others are excluded.
Highest Level of Participation	Division Chief, Training Manager, Affirmative Action Officer, Department Psychologist, others of importance.	Patrol Division head, Training Manager, others as needed.
Program Duration	Varies, but approximately 14 weeks training and evaluation.	One week integration (optional), 12 weeks training and 3 weeks evaluation.
Limbo Period(s)	First two weeks of program. First week is virtual ride-along, second is training and feedback. No evaluation during this period.	First week of program is the Integration Phase, which prepares the trainee for the program.

Rating Frequency	Daily, other than in limbo period.	Weekly problem-solving coaching and training critiques by the trainee and the PTO, midterm/final evaluations, PBL exercise evaluations.
Deployment Status of Trainee	Never assigned beyond control of FTO; call requiring two officers results in second unit dispatched.	Same.
Shift Assignment	Rotated for exposure to cross-section of service demands, citizens and community.	Trainees remain on day shift and swing shift (flexible) as problem-solving resources are more available, activity generally higher. This leads to more training opportunities.
Holdover Policy (Extension of Stay in Program)	Yes, if problem can be corrected.	Program is flexible and includes remedial training as integral component. "Failing forward" concept is central to training philosophy.
Compensation and Recognition	5% increase while trainee is in the program, ending at the 14th week.	Subject to local requirements.
Geographic Location for Assignment	One patrol district, continuous exposure to FTOs.	This model encourages geographic accountability facilitated by assignment and neighborhood portfolio problems.

Trainee Task List (a.k.a. Weekly Training Guide, Rookie Book)	Broken into week-by-week segments.	Training matrix consisting of core competencies that provide flexibility in learning opportunities.
Periodic Objective Tests	Weekly, on previous week's material in Task List (Training Guide).	Ongoing weekly PBL exercises, midterm and final evaluations, and reports.
Postacademy Training	In-house Academy following graduation from regional training center.	Same, plus PBL orientation.
The Validity Issue	Demand answered by Daily Observation Report (DOR).	Training criteria based on Job Task Analysis and contemporary policing philosophy (COPPS, PBL).
The Reliability Issue	Demand answered by DOR.	Reliability enhanced by continuity of training and evaluation, commitment of the PTO and adult learner, and independent evaluators.
Accreditation Standards	Traditional FTO model used as foundation for accreditation standard.	Exceeds accreditation standards.
Rotation Between FTOs	FTO (usually 14-week program): **1st 2nd 3rd 4th** (2)+2 4 4 2	PTO (15- or 16-week program): **Int 1st Mid 2nd Final** 1 6 1 6 2

"Evaluation-Only" Phase	Last two weeks of program. No training, but feedback follows each assignment.	One-week midterm evaluation and two-week final evaluation completed by independent evaluator. Evaluation is primary purpose, but learning continues.
Biweekly Meetings (a.k.a. Biweekly Evaluation Sessions)	9/10 shifts and team policing approach allows for overlap shift and minimal overtime expense.	Same.
Supervisory and Management Review of FTO Performance and Trainee Progress	Essential to ensure objectivity and standardization.	Same, plus Board of Evaluators (BOE).
Multiple Levels and Methods of Performance Evaluation	DOR by FTO, weekly report by supervisor. Biweekly report form. End of phase report. Trainee task list. Weekly tests and FTO worksheet.	Multiple levels and methods for application of training include weekly coaching and training reports, PBL community exercises, learning matrix, evaluation phases and BOE.
Functional Termination Authority	Vested in the FTOs and their immediate supervisor.	PTO, BOE and Program Coordinator.

Criteria and Methods Used to Select FTOs	Volunteers desired. Application, Oral Board Interview, supervisor's recommendation, experience as teacher/supervisor, performance and discipline records reviewed, police experience, positive role model, good communications skills.	PTOs and Police Training Evaluators (PTEs) selected based on community skills, problem-solving skills, commitment to COPPS, knowledge of resources, interest in adult learning techniques.
Training FTO Program Personnel	Five-day course for FTOs and supervisors. Emphasis on evaluation, documentation, learning, feedback, behavior, motivation, liability, supervision.	40-hour course emphasizing PBL, COPPS, adult learning, program structure application and evaluation, liability, leadership, ethics.
Supervisor and Command Staff Training and Selection	Similar to that of FTO.	Same as that of PTOs and PTEs.
Evaluation of FTO	By trainee at end of each rotation. By supervisor at end of each cycle. At the End of Probation Board.	Conducted by PTO supervisor, BOE and trainee.
Resignation and Termination Rates, Affirmative Action Interests	Approximately 25% in early years, 7–10% more recently. No adverse impact. EEOC Guideline 1607.5a applicable.	To be measured.

Adapted from "Key Elements," first developed by R. A. Allen and M. D. Roberts, Ph.D. In *The Field Training Concept in Criminal Justice Agencies*, by G. F. Kaminsky. Englewood Cliffs, N.J.: Prentice Hall,2001.

ABOUT THE AUTHORS

Daniel T. Albright is a 15-year veteran of the San Diego Police Department. Currently assigned to the Vice Section as a detective, Albright previously was assigned to the Mid-City area as a generalist detective for four years. In 1998, while assigned as a juvenile detective, he began extensive research on graffiti in the San Diego area. That research served as a catalyst for a problem-solving effort that received the Herman Goldstein Award at the 2000 POP Conference in San Diego, California. Albright lives in Santee, California, is married and has four children. He received his bachelor's degree in organizational studies from Bethel College in St. Paul, Minnesota.

Joanne Archambault has been with the San Diego Police Department for 21 years, assigned to the Sex Crimes Unit for the last nine years. The Unit has 13 detectives and investigates approximately 1,000 felony sexual assaults in San Diego each year. From 1985 to 1988, Archambault served as a detective in the Child Abuse Unit; other assignments have included Internal Affairs, the Office of Equal Employment Opportunity, Patrol, Crimes Against Persons and Gangs.

Archambault first developed the curriculum for investigating child abuse for the San Diego Police and Reserve Academy in 1987. In 1991, she revamped the sexual assault curriculum at the San Diego Regional Law Enforcement Academy. She coauthored the San Diego County Sexual Assault Response Team (SART) Resource Pamphlet and produced a video on SART used as a training aid for professionals responding to sexual assault. Archambault also worked with the National Center for Women and Policing to develop the first national sexual assault training curriculum for law enforcement. She has published and coauthored articles on drug-facilitated sexual assault, nonstranger sexual assault risk-reduction, sexual assault investigations and DNA evidence in sexual assault cases. She has lectured extensively to multidisciplinary audiences on the successful investigation of sex crimes throughout the United States.

Daniel Bibel is program manager of the Massachusetts State Police Crime Reporting Unit, which collects and analyzes summary and incident crime data for the Commonwealth of Massachusetts. Bibel has been in charge of the Unit since 1988; prior to that, he was the director of the Commonwealth's Statistical Analysis Center. He received his master's degree from Northeastern University and has done postgraduate work at Rutgers University.

Bibel has been involved in the development and implementation of the National Incident-Based Reporting System for the past 12 years, on both the national and state level. He has organized several panels on the issue at meetings of the American Society of Criminology and has presented numerous talks about crime mapping and analysis using incident-specific crime data.

Diana Brensilber is director of the Massachusetts Statistical Analysis Center and director of research and evaluation for the Massachusetts Executive Office of Public Safety Programs Division. She has researched incident-based reporting analysis, community policing, police technology, juvenile crime, delinquency prevention, youthful offenders, domestic violence, Weed and Seed programs, and convenience store robbery. Brensilber currently supervises several federal grants, including the National Criminal History Improvement Program (NCHIP), the State Justice Statistics Program and the National Institute of Justice–funded Impact Evaluation of the Barnstable County Residential Substance Abuse Treatment Program.

Brensilber serves on the Executive Committee of the Justice Research and Statistics Association and co-chairs the Research and Evaluation Subcommittee of the Massachusetts Governor's Commission on Domestic Violence. She is an active participant of the Commonwealth's Racial and Gender Profiling Advisory Committee, VAWA Advisory Board and Sexual Assault Evidence Collection Advisory Committee. Brensilber received her bachelor's degree in criminal justice from Northeastern University and her master's degree in applied sociology from the University of Massachusetts.

Gerard Cleveland is an international consultant on police training to the Police Executive Research Forum (PERF) and the Department of Justice. A former police officer who has been involved in modern methods of education and training for more than a decade, Cleveland specializes in problem-based learning, Crime Prevention Through Environmental Design (CPTED) and police education. Cleveland also is a high school principal who developed nationally known school safety and violence-prevention programs with the Toronto Board of Education and has consulted with police agencies in the United States, Canada and Australia. Most recently, he is a developer and trainer of the new problem-based learning program for training police recruits.

Dan Cunius is a 12-year veteran with the Charlotte-Mecklenburg Police Department. He holds an associate's degree from Cape Fear Community College and a bachelor's degree from the University of North Carolina at Charlotte. He has been a field training officer and worked in Burglary Investigations. Cunius also has been awarded the Chief's Award for Excellence in Policing, Medal of Valor and Certificate of Commendation. He currently develops community-policing software for the department.

Jack Drown has been undersheriff for San Diego County Sheriff Bill Kolender since 1995. Drown began his law enforcement career in 1969 as a deputy sheriff for the San Diego County Sheriff's Department. He spent 21 years with the department, attaining the rank of assistant sheriff in 1986, before becoming Police Chief of Coronado, California, in 1991. Drown holds a bachelor's degree from San Diego State University and a master's degree from National University. He is a graduate of the FBI Academy and attended the Senior Management Institute for Police. Drown also is a past president of the San Diego County Chiefs' and Sheriffs Association. A lifelong resident of San Diego County, Drown lives in Encinitas, California, with his wife Colleen and their two children, Erin and Brent.

Donald Faggiani is executive director of the Wyoming Statistical Analysis Center for Rural Policy Studies at the University of Wyoming. Prior to that, Faggiani has been deputy director of research for the Police Executive Research Forum (PERF) in Washington, D.C., and director of the Virginia Statistical Analysis Center (SAC). Faggiani also is an adjunct faculty member of the University of Wyoming Criminal Justice Department. He holds a doctoral degree in public policy analysis from the University of Illinois at Chicago.

Faggiani has worked extensively with the FBI's National Incident-Based Reporting System (NIBRS) and is recognized as one of the leaders in research using NIBRS data. He currently is involved in two projects incorporating GIS information with NIBRS data; one examines the use of NIBRS for regional crime analysis, while the second examines the spatial patterns of repeat burglary and robbery victimization. Two of his most recent publications, "Robbery of Older Adults: A Descriptive Analysis Using the National Incident-Based Reporting System" (*Journal of Research and Policy* 1999) and "Using the National Incident-Based Reporting System for Strategic Crime Analysis" (*Journal of Quantitative Criminology* 1999) focus on the practical aspects of NIBRS for public policy. Faggiani also is co-principal investigator on a Bureau of Justice Statistics-funded project to develop an Incident-Based Reporting Resource Center for the World Wide Web.

Lorie A. Fridell is director of research at the Police Executive Research Forum (PERF). Prior to joining PERF in August 1999, Fridell was an associate professor of criminology and criminal justice at Florida State University. She has more than 15 years' experience researching such law enforcement issues as police use of deadly force, use of less-than-lethal weapons, police-minority relations, police pursuits, felonious killings of police and community policing. In addition to articles and chapters on these topics, she published a two-volume report with Tony Pate entitled *Police Use of Force: Official Reports, Citizen Complaints and Legal Consequences;* with Geoff Alpert, she coauthored *Police Vehicles and Firearms: Instruments of Deadly Force*. She is lead author on the recently completed PERF report *Racially Biased Policing: A Principled Response,* which guides law enforcement agencies in their response to both racially biased policing and the perceptions of racially biased policing.

Sheldon F. Greenberg chairs the Department of Interdisciplinary Programs at Johns Hopkins University's Police Executive Leadership Program. In addition, he serves as coordinator of the Mid-Atlantic Regional Community Policing Institute. Prior to joining Johns Hopkins University, Greenberg was associate director of the Police Executive Research Forum (PERF). He began his career as an officer in the Howard County, Maryland, Police Department;

during his tenure there, he served as a criminal investigator, public information officer, supervisor of records and information, and director of the police academy. Greenberg worked with the U.S. Marshals Service and U.S. Border Patrol in a variety of capacities and has been an instructor for the Maryland State Police, Maryland Community Policing Academy and Maryland Police Training Commission. He also is one of the founding members and past president of the Maryland Crime Prevention Commission.

Corinne Hard is a vice detective for the San Diego Police Department, where she has been employed for more than eight years. Prior to this, she was assigned to a problem-solving grant designed to form a partnership between the police department and the community in San Diego's Mid-City Division. Her work under the grant earned her the Herman Goldstein Award at the 2000 POP Conference in San Diego, California.

Hard also teaches police academy recruits problem solving and high-risk vehicle stops. She is a certified Crime-Free Multi-Housing trainer, Police Cadet advisor and Field Training Officer and has conducted training in leadership and organizational change for the past 10 years for an outside consultant. She also has conducted training for visiting agencies, including the Sacramento City Council, a representative from Chile and the Regional Community Policing Institute in Sacramento, California. Hard holds a bachelor's degree in business management from San Diego State University.

Jerry Hoover is chief of the Reno, Nevada, Police Department. Hoover holds a master's degree in public administration from Harvard University, a master's degree in anthropology from Colorado State University and a bachelor's degree from San Diego State University. He began his police career in 1968 and has worked in the San Diego, California, Police Department (11 years); the Boulder, Colorado, Police Department (15 years); and the St. Joseph, Missouri, Police Department (three years). Hoover is a nationally recognized expert in field training officer concepts, critical incident/disaster management and the investigation of destructive religious cults/ritual crime. He also is an adjunct instructor at the University of Nevada, Reno.

Chuck Johnson is a 20-year veteran of the Charlotte-Mecklenburg Police Department. As an officer, he worked in Patrol for five years and Research and Planning one year; as a sergeant, he worked in Patrol as a shift supervisor, in Staff Inspections doing special projects and as a community-policing sergeant. He currently is captain of the Charlie One District and serves as a commander on the SWAT Team. He has been involved in community policing since its inception in Charlotte in 1991. Johnson holds a bachelor's degree in criminal justice/psychology from Michigan State University and a master's degree in criminal justice from the University of North Carolina at Charlotte. He is an adjunct instructor with the University of North Carolina at Charlotte, teaching classes on Community Policing and Criminal Justice Ethics.

Stuart Kirby is a chief superintendent with the Lancashire, England, Constabulary. He has 24 years of police experience in a variety of uniform and detective roles, currently commanding an area in the north of England with approximately 500 staff. Kirby uses his doctoral degree in investigative psychology to help police forces across the United Kingdom investigate serious sexual crimes against children. He also lectures at a number of universities in the north of England. Stuart has received the Tilley Award (the U.K. equivalent to a Herman Goldstein Award) for organizational support in problem-oriented policing for the past two years.

Suzanne P. Lindsay is an associate adjunct professor in the Division of Epidemiology at San Diego State University's Graduate School of Public Health. Dr. Lindsay's primary area of research involves the study of interpersonal violence, including family violence, spousal abuse, child abuse, youth violence and sexual assault. Her research projects include a comprehensive study of the health status of children in foster care in San Diego County, which is documenting the long-term health consequences of child abuse and neglect. Lindsay also coordinated a three-year, multisite international evaluation of interventions for the prevention of family violence in military families and has worked closely with the San Diego Police Department for the last five years studying sexual assaults reported to law enforcement.

Nigel Manning is crime reduction manager for the Stoke-on-Trent Division of the Staffordshire, England, Police. Recent reorganization of the Staffordshire Police established a Local Policing Unit (LPU) for the City Centre under Manning's command. Incorporating five shifts of officers, the Unit is responsible for the complete range of policing activities in the City Centre, 24 hours a day, seven days a week. Manning has increased police presence on the busiest nights to prevent violence and disorder; expanded community networks; enhanced weekly operations meetings among police, community groups and security staff; initiated the First Responder scheme to get immediate help to cardiac victims; and relaunched the City Centre Retail Crime Initiative.

Susan Pennell is director of criminal justice research at the San Diego Association of Governments (SANDAG). The division conducts program evaluations of crime and drug prevention and control strategies. She has conducted extensive research on drugs and crime, gangs, and juvenile delinquency and has been the San Diego site director for the Arrestee Drug Abuse Monitoring (ADAM) program. Pennell is principal investigator for evaluation of a multisite treatment replication program for methamphetamine addicts (MATRIX). She was a consultant for an evaluation of meth initiatives in six cities (funded by the Department of Justice's Office of Community Oriented Policing Services) and serves on San Diego's Methamphetamine Strike Force. She and Undersheriff Jack Drown have partnered on a number of occasions to address the importance of bringing research to the field. Pennell has a bachelor's and a master's degree in sociology from San Diego State University.

Jean Prince has been a police constable for 10 years. She has worked short assignments in Operations Special Events and Planning and Research. After several years working in "Skid Row," Prince was assigned to the Grandview-Woodland Community Policing Centre (GWCPC) in 1997. Recently reassigned to uniform patrol, Prince has a diploma of criminology from Douglas College and is working on a bachelor's degree in criminology.

Together with Valerie Spicer, Prince was a Herman Goldstein Award finalist in 1999. Their submission "Intersecting Solutions" dealt with problematic behaviors around the intersection of First Avenue and Commercial Drive in Vancouver. They also were finalists in 2000 for the project "Showdown at the Playground," highlighted in this book.

Eric Rost is a 12-year veteran with the Charlotte-Mecklenburg Police Department. He was one of the department's first Community Coordinators and worked as a bike officer. A deacon at the Fellowship Baptist Church of Huntersville, Rost received the Chief's Award for Excellence in Policing for the construction site theft reduction project highlighted in this book. He currently is assigned to the Charlie One District as a patrol officer.

Gregory Saville is a research professor at the University of New Haven and director of the Center for Advanced Public Safety Research. He was a police officer for nine years and is a formally trained urban planner. Saville specializes in problem-oriented policing, Crime Prevention Through Environmental Design (CPTED), leadership and training. He has consulted with communities working to develop safety programs and crime-prevention initiatives, including the designers of the Sydney 2000 Olympics, the Police Executive Research Forum (PERF), the Department of Justice, the Royal Canadian Mounted Police and municipal governments around the world. He currently is a developer and trainer of the new problem-based learning program for training police recruits.

Valerie Spicer has a bachelor's degree in fine arts from Concordia University and a master's degree in art history from the University of Montreal. She began her policing career in 1997 as civilian coordinator for the Grandview-Woodland Community Policing Centre (GWCPC), where she helped design and implement an extensive community survey establishing a baseline for community requirements. As coordinator, she also aided the community in solving quality-of-life issues. In November 1998, Spicer joined the Vancouver Police Department as a sworn member, graduating from the Justice Institute of British Columbia in 1999. She currently is assigned to uniform patrol and works on the bicycle unit.

Together with Jean Prince, Spicer was a Herman Goldstein Award finalist in 1999. Their submission "Intersecting Solutions" dealt with problematic behaviors around the intersection of First Avenue and Commercial Drive in Vancouver. They also were finalists in 2000 for the project "Showdown at the Playground," highlighted in this book.

David Tos has been a San Diego police officer for more than 12 years. He currently is a Community Relations Officer for the Mid-City Division, which—with more than 36 different languages spoken—is the most diverse area of San Diego. Tos created the first Community-Based Relations Office in the nation, which is operated by citizens; he also has received two Herman Goldstein Awards. Tos teaches problem solving throughout the country and has published several articles for the Police Executive Research Forum (PERF). In addition, Tos worked on a Price Charities grant for two years and was instrumental in mobilizing and educating the community on problem-solving techniques that highlight citizens' role in quality-of-life issues.

In an effort to reduce youth violence, Tos created a youth bike team called K.I.C. (Kids in Control). K.I.C. members ride their bikes after school with police officers throughout their neighborhoods, which are high-crime areas. This provides a positive after-school activity and enables them to view law enforcement officers in a positive light. Members also help identify problem areas and work through issues using the SARA (Scanning, Analysis, Response, Assessment) model. Additionally, officers teach conflict-resolution skills and mentor the youths in scholastic areas. In conjunction with the City Attorney's Office, Tos teaches a class called Juveniles in Justice to elementary children; the curriculum teaches students the law and their rights, as well as their roles, as citizens.

ABOUT PERF

The Police Executive Research Forum (PERF) is a national professional association of chief executives of large city, county and state law enforcement agencies. PERF's objective is to improve the delivery of police services and the effectiveness of crime control through several means:

- the exercise of strong national leadership,

- the public debate of police and criminal issues,

- the development of research and policy, and

- the provision of vital management and leadership services to police agencies.

PERF members are selected on the basis of their commitment to PERF's objectives and principles. PERF operates under the following tenets:

- Research, experimentation and exchange of ideas through public discussion and debate are paths for the development of a comprehensive body of knowledge about policing.

- Substantial and purposeful academic study is a prerequisite for acquiring, understanding and adding to that body of knowledge.

- Maintenance of the highest standards of ethics and integrity is imperative in the improvement of policing.

- The police must, within the limits of the law, be responsible and accountable to citizens as the ultimate source of police authority.

- The principles embodied in the Constitution are the foundation of policing.

RELATED TITLES

To request a free catalog or order PERF publications, call toll-free **1-888-202-4563**. A full listing of PERF publications can also be found at *www.policeforum.org*.

Problem-Oriented Policing: Crime-Specific Problems,
Critical Issues and Making POP Work (Volume 3)
Corina Solé Brito and Eugenia E. Gratto, eds., 2000, 246 pp.
Product #846, ISBN#1-878734-72-5
PERF Members: $27, Nonmembers: $30
The third in the problem-solving series, this book focuses on emerging issues in addressing community problems. It focuses on such issues as hate crimes, stalking, crime in public housing, public disorder and other issues of concern to police problem solvers.

Problem-Oriented Policing: Crime-Specific Problems,
Critical Issues and Making POP Work (Volume 2)
Corina Solé Brito and Tracy Allan, eds., 1999, 412 pp.
Product #840, ISBN#1-878734-70-9
PERF Members: $26, Nonmembers: $29
The second in the problem-solving series, this book focuses on emerging issues in addressing community problems. It focuses on such issues as domestic violence, repeat burglaries, the role of investigations in community policing, crime mapping and other issues of concern to police problem solvers.

Problem-Oriented Policing: Crime-Specific Problems,
Critical Issues and Making POP Work (Voume 1)
Tara O'Connor Shelley and Anne Grant, eds., 1998, 442 pp.
Product #831, ISBN#1-878734-60-1
PERF Members: $24, Nonmembers: $27
This publication is the first in a series that highlights information shared by practitioners and academicians with expertise in crime-specific problems, critical issues and practices, and the challenges of making problem solving work. Chapters include police problem solv-

ing for burglary, gangs, alcohol, domestic violence, guns, citizen over-
sight, fear in schools, criminal investigations and myriad other issues. Problem solving as it relates to zero tolerance, personnel
performance, criminal investigations and other strategies are also
discussed. The volume is ideal for academic classroom use, police
training and law enforcement promotional reading exams.

Mapping Across Boundaries: Regional Crime Analysis
Nancy LaVigne and Julie Wartell, 2001
Product #847, ISBN# 1-878734-74-1
Member/Nonmember Price: $20
Mapping Across Boundaries: Regional Crime Analysis addresses the obstacles and answers in developing regional crime mapping. The 130-
page report is a primer for police agency personnel and students of
mapping who want to enhance crime control and prevention efforts.
The book discusses how cross-boundary mapping can better reveal
hot spots of crime that occur along jurisdictional boundaries or identify serial crimes by offenders operating in neighboring jurisdictions.
The book provides guidance through case studies on a range of regional mapping models—from central archiving systems to ambitious
multiagency consortia with common database structures and GIS plat-
forms. This practical guide outlines for each case model how the
mapping effort began; how it was implemented; decisions regarding
software, hardware, data sharing.

Crime Mapping Case Studies: Successes in the Field (Volume 2)
Nancy LaVigne and Julie Wartell, eds., 2000, 140 pp.
Product #841, ISBN #1-878734-71-1
PERF Members: $18, Nonmembers: $20
This second Police Executive Research Forum (PERF)–National Institute of Justice Crime Mapping Research Center (CMRC) volume of
crime mapping case studies meets increasing demands for practical
information on how crime mapping technologies can be applied to
community and police agency problems. It highlights such issues as
gun violence, drug crackdowns, neighborhood watch efficacy, identifying serial suspects, sex offender registrant compliance, gang suppression, police agency redistricting/staffing and many more. Written
by practitioners, this volume is a must-read for students, police pro-

fessionals, policymakers and others interested in accurate information that supports crime control and community policing. It aids in suspect apprehension and prosecution; and improves law enforcement operations.

Crime Mapping Case Studies: Successes in the Field (Volume 1)
Nancy LaVigne and Julie Wartell, eds., 1998, 144 pp.
Product #834, ISBN #1-878734-61-X
PERF Members: $15, Nonmembers: $17
PERF and the CMRC collaborated in this volume to highlight various criminal justice agencies' successes with applying mapping to their problem-solving, prevention and enforcement efforts. The book encourages agencies' use of crime mapping and offers ideas on various ways to apply geographic information systems (GIS) and mapping. Readers can apply the case studies' approaches to their own jurisdictions.

Crime in the Schools:
Reducing Fear and Disorder with Student Problem Solving
Dennis J. Kenney and T. Steuart Watson, 1998, 236 pp.
Product #830, ISBN #1-878734-58-x
PERF Members: $20, Nonmembers: $23.95
More metal detectors, school security personnel and other target-hardening approaches alone fail to make our schools safer. *Crime in the Schools* provides a student-oriented response that builds on the success of police problem-solving efforts. The authors outline a tested curriculum that empowers students to make creative uses of school, student, faculty and police resources to combat the fear and disorder problems many experience during the school day. The School Safety Program applies the police problem-solving model, used successfully in community policing efforts nationwide, to school situations.

How to Recognize Good Policing
Jean-Paul Brodeur, ed., 1998, 272 pp.
Product #833, ISBN #:0-7619-1614-8
Member/Nonmember Price: $27.95
Copublished with SAGE publications, this book is divided into four parts. Part I provides a general overview of community and problem-

oriented policing. Part II is comprised of five chapters that specifically address issues in the assessment of police performance that include: the assessment of individual police performance; the problems
raised by making an evaluation; the role of the public in community
policing through participation in beat meetings, neighborhood watch
schemes, and public surveys to determine satisfaction levels. Part III
of this book addresses organizational change and its assessment. It
also includes a portion devoted to a summary of exchanges that occurred between chapter authors, police professionals and others involved in the areas of security. This book concludes with future
perspectives on increasing roles for private security agencies, hybrid
agencies and community involvement in civil policing.

Information Management and Crime Analysis:
Practitioners' Recipes for Success
Melissa Miller Reuland, ed., 1997, 152 pp.
Product #819, ISBN #1-878734-48-2
Member/Nonmember Price: $21
In *Information Management and Crime Analysis: Practitioners' Recipes for
Success,* police practitioners from around the country discuss ways to
manage police information to meet a variety of needs, from crime
analysis to community awareness. Chapters cover crime information,
database structures, administrative crime analysis, use of information technologies to assist investigations and tactical planning, how
crime analysts can use computer mapping to identify "hot spots,"
and decentralization of information to beat officers and citizens.

Why Police Organizations Change: A Study of Community-Oriented Policing
Jihong Zhao, 1996, 140 pp.
Product #811, ISBN #1-878734-45-8
PERF Members: $16.95, Nonmembers: $18.50
Why do police organizations change? What prompts them to make
the shift to community-oriented policing? In *Why Police Organizations Change,* Jihong Zhao addresses the various factors in both
the internal and external environment that prompt a police organization to adopt innovative approaches to policing. Such factors
range from managerial tenure and personnel diversity to local
political culture and community characteristics.

The Nature of Community Policing Innovations:
Do the Ends Justify the Means?
Jihong Zhao and Quint Thurman, 1996, 24 pp.
Product #810, ISBN #1-878734-46-6
PERF Members: $5.95, Nonmembers: $6.50
In *The Nature of Community Policing Innovations,* authors Jihong Zhao
and Quint Thurman use James Thompson's theory of organizational change as a theoretical framework to investigate the core
mission of American policing. They first examine the prioritization
of police functions and go on to address the relationship between
those priorities and the means used to achieve them, particularly
as they relate to community policing.

Themes and Variations in Community Policing:
Case Studies in Community Policing
PERF, 1996, 92 pp.
Product #809, ISBN #1-878734-42-3
PERF Members: $14.95, Nonmembers: $16.50
Supported through a grant from the National Institute of
Justice, *Themes and Variations in Community Policing* offers six examples of how community policing has been developed and applied by police agencies throughout North America. Each case
study provides the historical context in which community policing has emerged, the specific steps the police agency has taken
to implement it, and frank insights from police personnel, city
officials and citizens regarding this modern approach to policing.

Managing Innovation in Policing:
The Untapped Potential of the Middle Manager
William A. Geller and Guy Swanger, 1995, 204 pp.
Product #803, ISBN #1-878734-41-5
PERF Members: $24.95 , Nonmembers: $27.50
The conventional wisdom holds that middle managers are
almost inevitably obstacles to strategic innovation, including com-
munity policing. In *Managing Innovation in Policing,* however, authors
Geller and Swanger argue that, when properly motivated and sup-
ported, police middle managers have been and can be key players in
policing reform. This book includes case studies of successful middle

managers and suggestions for how police senior leaders, city officials and others can help position middle managers to voluntarily,
proactively and effectively help implement community policing. *Managing Innovation in Policing* has become a popular text for community
policing training courses.

Dispute Resolution and Policing:
A Collaborative Approach Toward Effective Problem Solving
Ron Glensor and Alissa Stern, 1995, 16 pp.
Product #007
PERF Members: $5, Nonmembers: $5.50
Today's police are called upon to handle an increasingly diverse
array of community problems, some of which they lack the authority or expertise to resolve. Consequently, some law enforcement agencies have turned to dispute resolution as a means for
working with professionals from other fields to develop new problem-solving strategies. In *Dispute Resolution and Policing,* authors
Glensor and Stern discuss dispute resolution techniques and use
case studies to illustrate how some agencies have successfully
used dispute resolution to address recurring problems.

Using Research: A Primer for Law Enforcement Managers
John E. Eck and Nancy La Vigne, 1994, 180 pp.
Product #045, ISBN #1-878734-33-4
Member/Nonmember Price: $19
Using Research, now in its second edition, remains the only research
text specifically tailored to police audiences. Authors John Eck and
Nancy La Vigne provide a comprehensive introduction to the research
process, from defining the problem to designing the research, from
analyzing the data to reporting the findings. They also provide criteria for judging others' research and a listing of information sources.
The second edition is updated to reflect changes in technology and
in the nature of policing itself. Anyone interested in evaluating police
practices will want to add this book to his or her collection.

Notes